HUB HEROES

REVEALING PROFILES OF BOSTON SPORTS LEGENDS ...AND MORE

CHRISTOPHER DALY

TO MY LATE PARENTS,

Daniel Daly, Corporal, U.S. Marines in World War II,
and
Ellen (Crahan) Daly, the perennial rock of our family

Each of whom qualify as a hero in their own way

TABLE OF CONTENTS

INTRODUCTION

WE AMERICANS HAVE long had a fascination with sports and the heroes that stride through arenas and stadiums like Greek gods, leaving mere mortals like us in awe of their talents.

For many of us, this fascination traces to our childhood, a simpler and more carefree time when a major dilemma on a summer day was whether we would play baseball or basketball, and what other kids in the neighborhood could be rounded up for a pick-up game.

It was also a time when we would imagine ourselves as giants of sports, standing at home plate with two outs in the bottom of the ninth and swatting a walk-off homer, or flinging a last-second shot that swishes through the net to give our team a victory. How many times have we counted down the clock before we let a basketball fly for a certain two points and victory before an imaginary cheering crowd?

Unfortunately, only a few athletes get to actually experience those kinds of events. These real-life heroes get the accolades, and also feel the downside of fame that comes with being a celebrity in a sports-mad city. Pressures that come with intense media scrutiny, demands for time from autograph-seeking fans, along with the expectation that they perform at a high level in every game in which they play can be the less attractive aspects of a superstar's existence.

Hollywood has immortalized mythic athletic feats, both true and fictional, on many occasions.

The movie *Hoosiers* is based on a real-life story of a team from a small Indiana high school team which beat the odds and won the state championship by mounting a comeback culminated by a last-second game-winning shot. Indiana native Larry Bird authored two buzzer-beaters in consecutive games to lead the Boston Celtics to victory and made many clutch shots in the closing moments of championship games.

In *Cinderella Man*, Russell Crowe portrays James J. Braddock, who rose from the Depression bread lines to defeat reigning heavyweight champion Max Baer, an overwhelming favorite, and win the title. Rocky Marciano wrote his own Cinderella story, emerging from a working-class Brockton, Massachusetts neighborhood to knock out highly regarded heavyweight champion Jersey Joe Walcott with a devastating punch to capture the coveted title.

Roy Hobbs, the fictional hero portrayed by Robert Redford in *The Natural*, clouts a monstrous game-winning homer that demolishes a bank of lights atop a tower in right field to deliver the pennant for the New York Knights. Mickey Mantle knew all about titanic home runs, having hit the longest tape-measure job in baseball history—565 feet. He was "The Natural" in real life.

For anyone who writes biographically about these heroes, it's vital to provide some little-known, surprising facts to give the reader a better idea of what they were really like and give a fuller picture of their lives. I hope I have succeeded in that regard.

This book is a collection of no-holds-barred profiles and commentary drawn mostly from my interviews—many one-on-one—with legendary athletes, as well as one iconic sports broadcaster. I've added interesting facts gleaned from historical research to bring my subjects into sharper focus. In summary, this book is a combination of memoir, biography, and sports history.

I have always enjoyed writing about people's lives. It's always a kick when I discover a clue about what makes someone tick. For instance, Bob Cousy's description of what he did to prepare for a big road game—including the belief that a player should never bring his family—is very revealing. And his comments condemning some of the unsavory practices of big-time college athletics that he witnessed during his tenure as head coach at Boston College could have been made yesterday, in light of recent basketball scandals at the University of Louisville and elsewhere.

With the exception of two entirely new chapters, these profiles are revised, updated, and expanded versions of articles written during my 12-year tenure on the staff of the *Fitchburg-Leominster Sentinel & Enterprise,* a daily newspaper in Central Massachusetts, where I served as a sportswriter and editor. I added new chapters on Marciano and Jack Chesbro because, as you'll see, I have a personal connection to these legendary figures and can lend a unique perspective.

Though most of these men have a strong identification with Boston, all but Bird have connections to New York. Cousy played high school ball in Queens. Celtics announcer Johnny Most grew up in the Bronx, went to Brooklyn College, and also broadcast New York Knicks and football Giants games, as well as those of the Brooklyn Dodgers. Marciano, who was raised near Boston in the city of Brockton, trained in New York City and at Grossinger's, the former Catskills resort. He also fought four of his six heavyweight title defenses in New York, three at Yankee Stadium and one at the Polo Grounds.

Carl Yastrzemski was a high school baseball and basketball star on Long Island. Wade Boggs, Roger Clemens, and Johnny Sain all played for the Yankees later in their careers.

This Boston-New York commonality adds an interesting twist to the collection of legends found in this volume. These two cities will be forever intertwined in heated sports rivalries, and most of these heroes saw the rivalries from both sides.

Of the 10 legends profiled, only half are still alive: Cousy, Bird, Yastrzemski, Boggs, and Clemens. All 10 made a lasting impression on their sports.

As a New York native born on Long Island who moved to Massachusetts at age 12, I've experienced allegiances to teams from both cities, enabling me to write both as a sports historian and as a fan.

If any of the images of these sports legends are murky to you now, I hope by the time you finish this book these images will be much clearer and give you a new perspective on these gifted men.

"If I had to do it over again,
I couldn't imagine playing anywhere but Boston."

—Bob Cousy at his retirement ceremony

CHAPTER 1

BOB COUSY

I had the opportunity to spend time with Bob Cousy in 1988 when I was among a small group of sportswriters to interview him at a Worcester, Massachusetts bookstore as he promoted his book, *Bob Cousy and the Celtic Mystique*. It had been three decades since he wrote his first memoir, titled *Basketball Is My Life*, with Al Hirshberg.

Cousy played on six Celtic NBA championship teams, was named NBA Most Valuable Player in 1957, and was a 13-time All-Star. A marvelous passer, he led the league in assists eight times. Cousy was elected to the Naismith Basketball Hall of Fame in 1971 and named to the NBA's 50th Anniversary Team in 1996.

The New York native starred at Andrew Jackson High School in St. Albans, Queens before joining a Holy Cross team that won the 1947 NCAA championship during his freshman season. He was a first team All-American in his senior year of 1950. The story that opens this chapter, which gives the full inside story of the draft that made Dave Cowens a Celtic, never appeared in the memoir that he was promoting.

1

"Houdini Of The Hardwood" Reflects On His Career

BOB COUSY CAN only marvel at how his former coach, the late Red Auerbach, built the Celtics into a championship organization. One move directly affected his pro coaching career when he guided the Cincinnati Royals, who later became the Kansas City-Omaha Kings and eventually the Sacramento Kings.

The Royals needed a big man. Veteran Connie Dierking was past his prime and Cousy had his eye on Dave Cowens, who was playing for Florida State. "The year Cowens came out the people didn't know about Cowens, but all the insiders knew about him," Cousy said. "The scouts knew he was going to be a player. They weren't sure if it was going to be as a center or forward, but whatever position, he had talent. We desperately needed a center and there were only two coming out that year, Cowens and Sam Lacey."

Actually, there's was another big man in the 1970 draft that he liked, but he knew he would likely be picked first, St. Bonaventure's Bob Lanier. The Detroit Pistons, who owned the top pick, did just that. Michigan's Rudy Tomjonavich and LSU's Pete Maravich were the next two players selected.

Cousy had scouted Lacey—a 6-foot, 10-inch center from New Mexico State—and had decided there was a huge difference between Lacey and Cowens. "I went to see Sam play two or three times and said to myself, 'Oh God, we don't want THAT guy.' "

That year the Celtics had the fourth pick, with the Royals picking next. Cousy asked Auerbach what player the Celtics were going to choose. Auerbach responded that Lacey would be the Celtics' pick. "Jesus, I was getting down on my knees every night hoping that was so," Cousy said.

When draft day arrived and the Celtics picked Cowens instead, a deflated Cousy saw his plans go up in smoke. "Man, that was the low point of my coaching career at that point," he said. "So we had to pick Lacey."

A year later, Cousy got more insight into why Auerbach changed his mind. He was playing golf with Ernie Barrett, who played briefly for the Celtics and was athletic director at the University of Kansas. Barrett had attended a Royals game against the Bucks the previous night in which Lacey played well.

"Sam used to get himself up a half dozen times a season, primarily against (Kareem Abdul-) Jabbar," Cousy said. "So he plays super against name centers in the league. The problem is there are only one or two name centers in the league, meaning he plays well in six games and mediocre to poor in the rest." In the game Barrett saw, Lacey outplayed Jabbar and the Royals won.

The next day during their golf match, Barrett told him a story that concerned the night before that disappointing draft day a year before. "I got to be honest with you," he told Cousy. "I'm losing it because I saw Lacey play repeatedly in college. And I not only didn't think he could play the way he did last night, I didn't think he could make the league. I really didn't think he could make the league. As a matter of fact Arnold (Auerbach) called me in the middle of the night the night before the draft and asked me what I thought of Lacey." Cousy had to restrain himself from hitting Barrett with his golf club.

For Cousy, there was no question in his mind that Auerbach's late night phone call had influenced his draft selection "He told us Lacey. There was no reason for him to lie to us. There's no question he relied on Ernie's word, which is probably just as well because if I had gotten Cowens I might still be coaching right now."

Cowens went on to share Rookie of the Year Honors with Portland's Geoff Petrie, won the league's MVP award in '73, and was inducted into the Hall of Fame. He was also named in 1996 to the NBA's 50th Anniversary Team.

Actually, Lacey wasn't really the draft bust that either Barrett or Cousy anticipated. He averaged 12.2 points and 12.5 rebounds per game in his first six seasons. There were only seven other players in the league to do that during that span, including draft classmates Lanier and Cowens. Lacey had his best season the year Cousy stepped down early, '73-'74, averaging 14 points and 13.4 rebounds per game. The next season he was named to the All-Star team.

Lacey had 14 assists in a game twice. When he died in 2014 at 66, only two other centers had accomplished that in the previous 40 years: Joakim Noah and Bill Walton. He played in more games than any members of his draft class.

There was another player Auerbach selected in that draft that paid future dividends. North Carolina's Charlie Scott had already signed with the American Basketball Association's Virginia Squires when the Celtics picked him in the seventh round. When Scott wanted to jump to the Phoenix Suns in 1972, they had to go through Boston to acquire his rights.

The Suns traded forward Paul Silas to the Celtics in exchange. Silas was a member of Celtics championship teams in '74 and '76. Scott was also a key contributor to the '76 title, as he was acquired for Paul Westphal prior to that season. Scott was inducted into the Hall of Fame in 2018.

Auerbach drafted junior Larry Bird as the sixth pick in 1978, knowing that Bird planned to play his senior year at Indiana State and wouldn't join the Celtics until the following season. Sharpshooting Brigham Young University guard Danny Ainge, who would later assume Auerbach's job, gave the impression that he was going to play professional baseball with the Toronto Blue Jays. Yet, Auerbach drafted him and Ainge joined the Celtics.

Cousy looks back at the moves Auerbach made with awe and wonder. "There are too many things that he pulled off, far out stuff, that took massive chutzpah," he said. "He sat there waiting for Bird coming off the worst year they had. He himself had no idea Bird would become as good as he was. He bit the bullet on Ainge when he convinced the world he wasn't going to play (basketball)."

Then there was the infamous Bob McAdoo trade in 1978. Spurred on by his former Miss America wife Phyllis George, then Celtics owner John Y. Brown gave up three first round draft picks to the New York Knicks for McAdoo, a good-shooting forward who had once been the league's Most Valuable Player. Auerbach wasn't consulted, leaving him to seriously consider leaving the Celtics organization. But then Auerbach turned that situation around a year later.

In 1980, Auerbach traded McAdoo to Detroit for the right to sign Pistons' swingman M.L. Carr and also acquired two first round Pistons' draft picks. One of those picks was the 13th overall that Detroit had acquired from Washington. The other pick was Detroit's own pick, which ended up as the first overall after the Pistons won only 16 games. Auerbach traded that pick to the Golden State Warriors as well as the 13th overall pick in exchange for center Robert Parish and Golden State's pick, the third overall. Auerbach used that pick to select Minnesota forward Kevin McHale.

Both Parish and McHale are members of the Basketball Hall of Fame and were also named to the league's 50th anniversary team. Purdue center Joe Barry Carroll, the player the Warriors selected first, showed early promise but faded as an NBA player later in his career, acquiring the nickname "Joe Barely Cares." Mississippi State's Rickey Brown, selected by the Warriors with the 13th pick, played five undistinguished years in the NBA before taking his game to Europe.

Referring to Auerbach's master stroke following the trade of McAdoo to the Celtics, Cousy said, "The next year McAdoo became M.L. Carr, which just one-for-one would have been a good trade. But he not only became M.L. Carr, he became Kevin McHale and Robert Parish. And that's got to be the most obscene trade in the league."

Cousy said that was the start of the Bird era. "It would never have been in place, as great as Bird is, if he didn't have McHale and Parish along with him. There are so many variables in judging talent. Auerbach has hit the mark too often." Cousy regards Bird as the greatest basketball player ever, which is quite a statement when one considers the legend who played center on Cousy's NBA championship teams.

As Celtics boss in 2013, Ainge engineered a trade that would have made the old master proud, greatly aiding the Celtics in the rebuilding process to make the team into a contender again. He fleeced the New Jersey Nets by trading aging stars Paul Pierce and Kevin Garnett, along with veteran role player Jason Terry to New Jersey for the Nets' 2014, 2016, and 2018 first round picks, with the right to swap picks in 2017. The Celtics also agreed to take on four marginal Nets players as the team moved to shed some salaries.

New Jersey never expected those picks to be high in the draft, but the Nets went into a deep nosedive and became one of the worst teams in the league. The Celtics would up with the third overall pick (University of California swingman Jaylen Brown) in 2016 and the first in 2017 (when they traded down two spots, took Duke forward Jason Tatum at No. 3, and, for their trouble, acquired another potentially high future selection). The trading of the Nets' 2018 first round pick to the Cleveland Cavaliers shortly before the start of training camp in 2017 was a key piece in the deal that brought All-Star guard Kyrie Irving to Boston.

The Brooklyn trade has been called "the gift that keeps on giving."

Cousy remembers the day when Auerbach first told him about Bill Russell. "He came to me and told me about Russell in December of Russell's last year (in college). He said, 'I've got a guy that we're going to get that's going to change it all around,' or words to that effect. We didn't take him seriously. He had to do a lot of maneuvering to get Russell and there was luck involved in the way he got him. But again, he did not know how effective Russell would become. But he knew he was going to provide rebounding and defense. So he's been right too often. But chance does play a role."

The late night phone call to Barrett about his opinion of Lacey was standard operating procedure for Auerbach. "He's relied on a lot of personal relationships," Cousy said. "He's always had people. He called Bones McKinney and Bones said there's a guy down here you ought to look at named Sam Jones. And he drafted him just on what Bones said. And Sam was inducted into the Hall of Fame."

Cousy didn't have any plans or inclination to coach an NBA team when he retired. Instead, he became the coach at Boston College, where he had some success between 1963 and '69, qualifying for the NCAA tournament in two of his three final years. He had already informed BC that he wouldn't be returning when his agent told him the Royals were interested in him. But Cousy wasn't interested in *them*. The Royals were persistent.

"Somebody told Max Jacobs (brother of Bruins owner Jeremy) he ought to get a name coach and he started chasing me," Cousy said. "And he literally made an offer I couldn't refuse because I had no funds built up. And at that point we just got the Mickey Mouse pension put in for pre-1965 players a few months before. I had no savings. I had made $30,000 my last year. So at that point I think I was earning $15,000 at BC."

During this chase Cousy told his lawyer, "Get this guy off my back. I have no interest in professional coaching and certainly not in Cincinnati. Let's make an offer he's got to refuse." His attorney called him back the next day and said, "Pack your bags. You're going to Cincinnati." The Royals had agreed to pay him $100,000 a year, making him the first United States professional coach to earn that much.

The job allowed him to put some savings away during the next four years, but he believed that going into the job with that motivation may have affected his ability to make the commitment that was required. "Most of the time my wife stayed here, as well as my kids," he said. "So it wasn't a case of distractions. And the fact the team was losing. I don't know if we would have lost less if I had given it 120 percent or whatever. We were about a middle of the pack team."

Cousy woke up one morning and asked himself what he was doing there, so far away from family and friends, and decided he'd had enough. He resigned 22 games into his fifth season and headed home.

Cousy was tired of dealing with today's professional athlete. "We all do whatever we must do," he said. "If I had to continue to earn a living that way I would have done it. Thank goodness I had other options. I could generate income in other ways."

Even back in his first book, he was saying that there is an imbalance in our society. "There's something wrong here," he wrote.

"We're over-glorifying jocks and overpaying them while people are preparing to go to the moon and working on cancer cures and the average person never heard their name."

Cousy found that coaching was a natural transition for him when he retired from the Celtics. "You need an outlet when you are an extremely competitive person," he said. "Now I channel it into a little golf and tennis. But at that point where I was 35 I went into coaching. It doesn't give you the outlet you had as a player because as a player you can physically release all that pent-up energy and competitive desire you have and feel better about it. As a coach it gives you somewhat of a release but normally you're just sitting there."

He has many fond memories of his days at Boston College. The story goes that one reason Cousy chose Holy Cross over Boston College as a collegian was that Holy Cross had student dormitories and BC didn't at the time. He made many longtime friendships with his BC assistant coaches, one of them Gerry Friel, who coached for many years at the University of New Hampshire. Many of his former players also keep in touch.

Yet it wasn't all sweetness and light at Chestnut Hill for the former Celtic great. "It was then and is now a hockey and football school," he said. "Fine. That's their privilege. But I chose after six years not to continue fighting that battle and the recruiting battle."

Cousy said he found out what it takes to be a successful basketball coach at the Division I level, calling the recruiting process a dehumanizing one. "In order to be ultimately successful you've got to do things with these kids," he said. "Sit on their doorsteps, plead with them. And if you're really in some of these major programs you've got to go through all the nasty things that we all read about in terms of goodies.

"First, it's find them companions and then it's become find daddy a companion. Whatever button has to be pressed is pressed. There's so much money involved. So, again, I didn't have to do that. As much as I enjoyed the relationship, I said, 'Hey, there are easier ways.' I walked away." Cousy said the Royals offer didn't come until months later and didn't have anything to do with his BC departure.

Then he got to coach NBA players and got another education.

He spoke about a then recent story in the newspaper in which the Celtics' McHale talked about rearranging his priorities, saying his job would now come in second place to his family.

"That's all laudable, but I'll tell you what, it would be getting my attention," Cousy said. "I'd have him in explaining to me where exactly his priorities are because during those eight months I expect him to give me his complete attention. I'm thinking that you have to eliminate as many distractions as possible." McHale later became a coach and general manager. One wonders if his views changed.

Cousy was known for his extraordinary focus as a player. "People from time to time thought I was aloof, but when I got to the floor I wasn't going to acknowledge anyone, including my wife unless her skirt was on fire," he said. "Goddammit, focusing and concentration is so important. We talk about the Celtics taking their wives and kids to the finals. None of you would take your wife and kids to the office if you've got something meaningful to be done…This is what it's come to…I regret I didn't spend more time with my kids. Your career is the whole thing and unfortunately you divorce yourself too much from more important things as we look at it now. But that also is what makes you successful."

His need to focus like a laser beam on his opponent would lead him to attempt to block out the rest of the world prior to a big game. "When we got into L.A. I had my meals sent up," he said. "I'd put up the 'Do Not Disturb' sign on the telephone and I'd try to create this emotional frenzy within myself, so that by the time I got on the floor I didn't even want to shake hands with the guy I was going to play

"I would focus such a hatred on that individual, but you can't do that if you're taking your kids by the hand and going to visit Disneyland. If your wife and kids are there, you have a responsibility to say, 'What are you going to do today dear?' You're concerned. In my judgment, it's something that should be eliminated to some degree. They're home any time the team is home. They live at home. Do whatever you need to do to be a responsible parent but Jesus, when you're on the road it's different."

Cousy averaged 18.4 points, 7.5 assists, and 5.4 rebounds during his career. Along with his playing success, he also was instrumental in the founding of the NBA Players Association, which was recognized by the league's owners in 1957 after a three-year struggle, addressing long-held player grievances. He served as its first president.

The consummate playmaker, Cousy was known for being able to dribble well with either hand. A childhood accident involving a fall from a tree caused him to suffer a broken right arm. This mishap forced him to learn how to dribble with his left hand, a skill that became invaluable later on. As a boy, he had to learn a new language. His parents were French immigrants and he didn't speak English until the age of 6 after entering school. Both he and Russell bounced back from having been cut from their high school teams one year.

Did he regret not coaching the Celtics? "The timing was wrong each time," he said. "I think it was a mistake the first time around when Arnold (Auerbach) spoke to me about it and I would have had to coach Russ(ell), even though Russ and I had a good relationship. I think it was a master stroke naming him coach. By that time he had nine championships in his pocket."

Later in 1969 when Cousy was considering the Royals' offer, he talked to his old coach again. Auerbach asked if he could wait a year. Then he would name him as coach of the Celtics. Russell, the last active player on the team that Cousy played with, was expected to retire at the end of the season. But Auerbach wasn't in a position to offer him nearly as much as the Royals offered. "The way he looked at it, he was offering you a chance to coach *the Celtics,* not just some ordinary team." Cousy said.

The first decision not to coach the Celtics was consistent with his desire to avoid coaching players who had once been his teammates. He thought that it would impact his effectiveness because of the previous relationship. Now, he would be the guy blowing the whistle in practices. He didn't like the thought of it.

Although he had a good relationship with Russell, no relationship is perfect, and Cousy learned some things after he retired that indicated that the great center resented being passed over for some endorsements during the Celtics' championship years. "If you examine it more carefully and you say to yourself, 'Maybe that's so,' and if I had been Russell I would have had some resentment." The fact that

Cousy was white didn't hurt his chances of securing more endorsement opportunities. Remember that Martin Luther King's famous "I Have a Dream" speech took place the same year Cousy retired.

Continuing on that theme, he added, "Whenever you're on top, you're thinking that all the people love me. You don't relate to the normal natural jealousies that go on with a unit. So the next year they dedicate their season to winning without me. I was momentarily crestfallen. I just didn't understand it. Now, when I look back at it I realize that's a natural reaction. Plus, Auerbach used it to juice the troops up."

Though Russell might not have been getting the same amount of product sponsorships, Cousy wasn't exactly overwhelmed with those types of opportunities when he was playing. "I really didn't do that many commercials," he said. "They weren't using athletes in commercials as much as they do now. But I was the most visible NBA player, so if there was something available, I guess I got the most of it. But if there was a feeling present, coming back as a coach wouldn't have made it easy to develop the kind of relationship you need."

But coaching in the NBA was not a goal Cousy had when he retired as a player. "I really didn't have the burning desire to coach at the professional level," he said. "There are so few satisfactions. It's much more sophisticated now." For instance, Auerbach didn't have the opportunity to make use of the various video applications that coaches have available to them today in assessing teams. For years, Auerbach never had an assistant coach. A typical NBA coach today has at least two or three.

Cousy believes that it is much harder to turn around a poor NBA franchise than to invigorate a college program. "In college if you have a reasonable amount of knowledge and you are able to develop a relationship with the players, and the school gives you whatever cooperation that is necessary you should be able to go in and say, 'Within three to five years I'm going to give you a competitive program.' That doesn't mean Final Four, but you're going to go 18-7 or perhaps 20-5. And if you don't you haven't gotten the job done. If you bust your ass you'll find there are players out there you can attract if you work hard at it."

He continued, "But in the pros you can be the best damn coach in the world. You can work your tail off like Bill Fitch, who is a workaholic. He spends all night watching those films. You can have the most sophisticated scouting. You can spend all the money and know where every damn player is in the world, which it has come to that point, but when it comes time to make judgments, to make choices, it's left entirely to chance—where you finish, who drafts ahead of you is left to chance. It's a coin flip.

"One year Ralph Sampson, who turned out to be a pussy anyway, is the top pick, another year Kareem Abdul-Jabbar (then known as Lew Alcindor) was the first pick. Then you have to lower your sights."

Cousy himself was a prime example of how chance can be a factor in a player's career and a team's success. He had expected the Celtics would choose the local hero in the 1950 draft and was devastated when they chose a big man, Bowling Green's Charlie Share. Cousy was selected by the Tri-Cities Blackhawks, a team Cousy was unfamiliar with and didn't even know where they played home games. The team played in two Illinois cities, Moline and Rock Island, and also in Davenport, Iowa. Just as Cousy had resigned himself to playing there, he learned that Tri-Cities had traded him to the Chicago Stags, a franchise that folded prior to the next season.

The players from the Stags roster were dispersed around the league. As that process progressed, three remaining players—Max Zaslofsky, Andy Phillip, and Cousy—would be divided among the New York Knickerbockers, Philadelphia Warriors, and the Celtics. It was decided that the three names would be put into a hat, with each team drawing a name. Celtics owner Walter Brown picked first and he drew Cousy. And the rest is history. What if Brown had picked Zaslofsky or Phillip? So Cousy knew all about chance.

And working with young people at BC gave Cousy more satisfaction than dealing with the pro athlete in trying to get them to play what Cousy calls "a child's game." When a player has a guaranteed multi-million dollar contract it can be harder to get his attention, especially when a coach is making a fraction of what the player makes.

When Cousy announced his retirement in 1963, the Celtics held a tribute event honoring him that year before a packed and adoring

Boston Garden audience. Johnny Most, the longtime Celtics radio announcer, served as master of ceremonies. Of Cousy, he said, "I certainly have felt it a tremendous privilege to merely to be associated with this fellow in any small way."

Several speakers talked about their relationship with Cousy. Brown confessed to making one of the greatest errors in judgment an owner can make. "If you have a sinking feeling in your stomach and if Red does, you can imagine how I feel," he said. "I'm the guy who didn't want Bob Cousy. What a genius!"

Even though Cousy had been an outstanding college player, some coaches, including Auerbach, weren't sure he could become a successful NBA player. They thought he might just be a flashy ball-handler. Like in the case of Bird, Auerbach had no idea how much impact Cousy would make on his team. He was a small man—6 feet, 1 inches in a big man's game—and he couldn't run fast. He also had a playing weight of only 175 pounds.

But in Cousy's first book, he explained the physical attributes that more than offset those deficiencies and contributed to his success, describing himself as somewhat of a freak of nature. "I have unusually long arms and sharply sloping ape-like shoulders," he wrote. "And if you have ever noticed an ape, his arms are so long he can easily clasp them behind his back. So can I. I have huge ham-like hands, my fingers are long and strong, and I can grip a basketball like a baseball. I have tremendously powerful thighs, which give me the strength to run all night.

"My muscles are resilient, and I can stop and change direction quickly. And I have unusual peripheral vision. I can see more than most people out of the corners of my eyes. I don't have to turn my head to find out what's going on at either side. It sometimes appears that I'm throwing the ball without looking. I'm looking all right but out of the corners of my eyes."

During his remarks on Cousy Day, fittingly held on St. Patrick's Day, Brown told of a side of Cousy and his teammates that many had not heard. "Things weren't always so good with the Celtics, and one year they were so bad I couldn't pay them their playoff money. I didn't pay them for nearly a year. Bob never said a word. Neither did Ed Macauley, or Bob Brannum, Bill Sharman, Chuck Cooper, all those great guys. And they permitted the club by this action to exist. It was the greatest tribute ever paid to me, the greatest one I hope to ever have paid to me. Bob, I want to thank you for all the boys you represent. For 13 years you've been the Boston Celtics and boy they've got a lot to live up to."

Auerbach read a presidential citation from John F. Kennedy, then added, "Well, that was the president. Now, I've got something to say too. People often ask me how I am going to replace Bob (long pause)…That's my answer. It can't be done. I'm so happy for him this day. He deserves everything. There's nothing I really can say. Anything the Celtics, myself, can do for him later on we'll do. I know he'll help us along. It's just one of those things. I just want to thank you people for coming out here because that's 'Mr. Basketball.'"

The normally composed Cousy wiped away tears as he took the microphone. He summed up his time in Beantown this way: "If I had to do it over again, I couldn't imagine playing anywhere but Boston." A man shouting out from the crowd expressed the sentiments of those attending, "We love ya Cooz!"

He went on to help the Celtics win another NBA title in that year's playoffs. In the championship series against the Lakers, Cousy had to leave a game in Los Angeles after twisting an ankle. He later was able to return. But thinking that this might be the last time they saw him on the floor, the Laker fans rose in unison to applaud him, even though he had caused them to experience a lot of heartache during his career. "They are ALL standing," Most told his radio listeners. "They're ALL standing for 'Mr. Basketball.'"

Celebrating his 90th birthday this year, Cousy has split time between homes in Massachusetts and Florida. His beloved wife Missie died in 2013 after battling dementia. They raised two daughters, each of whom became teachers.

On Mount Saint James, near Holy Cross' Hart Center, is a statue of the "Houdini of the Hardwood," the man who led the Crusaders to its only national championship in 1947. Even when he was playing for the Celtics he lived in Worcester and he has continued to do so.

Whether it be in Worcester, Boston, or throughout the country, Cousy has made an enduring mark on the "child's game" he loves.

CHAPTER 2

LARRY BIRD

I interviewed Larry Bird in the spring of 1986, shortly before the second round of the NBA Eastern Conference playoffs. He had just finished a practice session at Hellenic College in Brookline, Massachusetts as the Celtics were preparing to face the Atlanta Hawks. The Celtics had just disposed of the Chicago Bulls in a three-game sweep, despite a playoff record 63-point performance by Michael Jordan in Game 2.

At this time, Celtics fans were optimistic about adding a 16th banner to the rafters at Boston Garden. This team was truly one of the greatest in Celtics history. It was also one of Bird's best seasons, resulting in his third and final league MVP award. He averaged 25.8 points, 9.8 rebounds and 6.8 assists.

The 1980 Rookie of the Year was named to the All-NBA First Team nine times in his career, was a 12-time All-Star, and a NBA Finals MVP twice. He led the Celtics to championships in 1981, '84, and '86, and also won an Olympic gold medal in 1992 as a member of the "Dream Team." Four years later, he was named a member of the NBA's 50th Anniversary Team.

Bird was inducted into the Basketball Hall of Fame in 1998. He coached the Indiana Pacers from 1997-2000 and has won the Coach of the Year Award. He was appointed President of Basketball Operations for the Pacers in 2003 and has also been a recipient of the Executive of the Year Award. After stepping down from the executive post in 2017, he still assists the team in an advisory role.

2 | Basketball's Most Complete Player

THERE WILL ALWAYS be debates about which basketball player is the greatest of all time. For me, the greatest player is the most complete player: Larry Bird.

No other player could do more things well on the basketball floor than the Celtics' forward. When one thinks of Michael Jordan and Lebron James, an image of an unstoppable scorer comes to mind. Magic Johnson provokes images of great passing, Bill Russell of rebounding and defense.

Some might argue that Bird is not even the best small forward of all time, giving James the nod. James is certainly a great player, but Bird was a more *complete* player. Bird was a better rebounder, while being fairly comparable in scoring and assists per game. He epitomized the team play the Celtics have been known for throughout the years. Bird was the total package. He could do it all.

Add to that a quality of mental toughness, fierce competitiveness, and unselfishness that were as legendary as his basketball skills and you have a player for the ages. That made him a very rare Bird indeed. It is doubtful we will see his like again.

Celtics great Bob Cousy wrote that Bird is "the greatest passing forward of all time" whose shooting range was "totally destructive to the opposition."

He is among the most beloved athletes in Boston sports history. Hub fans have seen a lot of great athletes through the years, but perhaps only Bobby Orr, David Ortiz, and Tom Brady can compete with Bird for the fans' affections.

Watching Bird reminds one of Orr. Both played the game at a different level from the other athletes in the game. The game just came easier to them. Frank Deford, the late great American sportswriter, once wrote that Bird seemed to see the game "in slow motion," while the others on the floor were operating at regular speed. How else to explain Bird's unbelievable passing skills. Legendary Celtic broadcaster Johnny Most said that Bird seemed to have "eyes in the back of his head" when making some passes.

If a player can be measured by the effect he has on the play of a team, the argument can be made that Bird is the greatest. Has one player caused such a dramatic reversal in a team's fortunes as Bird did in his first season? The Celtics owned a dismal 29-53 record the year prior to Bird's arrival. The 61-21 record in Bird's rookie season represented the greatest one-season turnaround in NBA history up until that time. The 1979-80 Celtics team held that distinction until the San Antonio Spurs jumped from 20 to 55 wins between 1997 and 1998 with the drafting of Tim Duncan and the return of All-Star David Robinson, who had been injured the previous year.

During his playing career, people would ask him, "Are you the greatest player ever?" Eventually he tired of the question, responding, "I say no, because I look at Wilt Chamberlain and Bill Russell and these other players. And right now there's no question I'm in the top five or 10 players in the league, but everybody's so close and everybody's got their own individual that they like. So why don't we put it all to rest and say, 'He's a good player and he's a good player, and if I was starting a basketball team I'd want them on my team,' instead of trying to pinpoint who's the best, because we'll never know."

For many years, the late Red Auerbach said that if he had to pick one player to start a team it would be Russell. Eventually, he changed his mind, picking Bird instead. And Russell won 11 championships.

Russell, whom many regard as the greatest player in the history of the league, said that he believed Auerbach's philosophy of team play fit perfectly with this own approach to the game.

Did Bird feel that coming to the Celtics helped him reach his basketball potential? "I have no idea," he said. "That's a tough question. The same thing could have happened somewhere else. I can't say the Celtics made me a great basketball player. You have to realize that the Celtics won 29 games the year before and with some additions that they didn't know—Dave Cowens came back and played well. They brought M.L. Carr in. The next year they made the trade for (Robert) Parish and (Kevin) McHale. They didn't know how them guys were going to be. If Robert played the way he did at Golden State we probably wouldn't have been very good at all. Nobody knew how Kevin was going to be. I think it was a lot of luck and a lot of good moves on Red's part."

True, those additions made a difference in the Celtics, but there is no question that Bird was the engine that powered the championship machine.

Bird is well aware that his grammar isn't always correct while speaking. A self-proclaimed "Hick from French Lick," the occasional fracturing of the English language seems to go along with the role. But he does catch himself sometimes. For instance, he'll say "ain't" and sometimes add "isn't" to correct himself immediately afterward.

In an era of athletes bringing attention to themselves, Bird was always quite content to share the glory. He made sure that other teammates got credit for a job well done. The joining of Parish, McHale, and Bird created perhaps the greatest front line in basketball history.

He has a special reverence for Dennis Johnson, who sadly died in 2007 at 52. Bird gave his reasons: "When you talk about bringing the ball up, defense, passing the ball, helping out on defense, we're talking about the total player. He was the best I ever played with."

Bird said that Johnson got a bad reputation prior to coming to Boston after playing in Seattle and Phoenix. "Everybody said back then D.J. would never fit in with the Celtics because they said he had a bad attitude. I have yet to see that. He's been a great player. Whoever said Dennis Johnson could be our point man? So I think it's the make-up of the individual that's important."

The word "legend" is tossed around frequently in the sports world, but few athletes really deserve that label. Bird is one of them. When telling some of the stories about Bird, one thinks of those told about the great Babe Ruth.

Consider this story by former Celtics Coach K.C. Jones, who remembered a timeout during a game with a few seconds left, and the Celtics needing a basket to win. Jones told the story at "Larry Bird Night" honoring the Celtics great at Boston Garden.

"I diagrammed a play and Larry said, 'The heck with the play coach. Case, give me the ball and tell all the other guys to get out of the way.' I said, 'Shut up Larry. I'm the coach here. Now Dennis, you take the ball out. Give it to Kevin and he'll throw it to Larry, and everybody get the hell out of the way.'

"Then true to his word in Phoenix he's standing in front of the Phoenix bench before the ball is thrown in and looks down at the guys on the bench and says, 'I'm getting the ball and I'm going to put it through the hoop. Watch my hand as I follow through.' The ball is thrown to Kevin. Kevin gets it to Larry, who fires it in the hoop and puts his hand in the air as he continues to the dressing room. Now that's what you call arrogance."

Many truly great players carry this arrogance around with them. It is something that comes along with the psychological make-up of many champions. Some athletes display this arrogance and breed animosity from players. Bird often displayed it in a way that drew admiration and awe from his peers.

It was this cockiness and self-assuredness that made him walk into the locker room at the All-Star game in Dallas in 1986 and ask the question, "Who's playing for second?" in the three-point shooting contest. Guess who pocketed $10,000 in winning the competition?

He was one of the greatest trash talkers of all the time, and the fact that he usually backed up his talk fueled a growing legend. One year when the Celtics were playing in Los Angeles the Lakers' Magic Johnson couldn't play due to an injury. Bird approached him before the game and advised him to sit back because he was going to put on a show for the Lakers star. Not surprisingly, he dominated in a Celtic victory.

The amazing thing about Bird is there are so many instances of him saying he's going to do something and doing just that. The proclamation to the Phoenix players was one of many instances he had accurately predicted the future to his opponents. It was reported that a teammate said that Larry was "into degree of difficulty," meaning he sometimes tried to purposely make things harder on himself to present more of a challenge to keep his interest. During the '86 season he started shooting more with his left hand, as if he was giving himself another challenge.

Where it can be said that Ruth called his shot during the 1932 World Series, it can also be said that Bird did the same thing many times.

Bird even challenged his own teammates. In a game against the Detroit Pistons, McHale seemingly couldn't miss. He kept piling up the points until he reached 56. With the Celtics comfortably ahead, Jones took McHale out of the game. The coach had asked McHale if he wanted to go back in the game later to attempt to reach 60 points, but he declined. Bird had encouraged him to do so, later telling him that he was going to try for 60 points someday. Less than two weeks later he did, scoring 60 against the Atlanta Hawks in a game played in New Orleans.

Last-second shots were his specialty. It was a pleasure to personally witness one of these miracles, which took place during a weekend game against the Portland Trailblazers. With about two seconds left, Bird took an inbound pass, dribbled into the corner and launched an off-balance shot from slightly behind the backboard. The 20-footer went through the net to the shock and disbelief of Clyde Drexler and the rest of the Portland players, resulting in euphoria among the Garden faithful. Remarkably, he scored a buzzer-beating jump shot to win the next Celtics' game, played in Hartford.

Perhaps the characteristic that endeared him to many fans was the fact that he didn't possess the awesome specimen of a body, remarkable speed, or many other attributes that a great player often possesses. He simply willed himself to greatness by pure dedication and hard work—a blue collar player. Many old-timers consider Bird a throwback to the players of an earlier era, a time when players were more fundamentally sound and dedicated to improving their abilities. As great as he was, Bird never stopped wanting to be better, dedicating himself each summer to adding another skill to his repertoire.

Asked whether he thought he was a better player at the time of the interview, as opposed to earlier in his career, he said he was better at his approach to the game, "Mentally, I know I'm better. There are no surprises anymore."

Being a white superstar in a largely black league also made him unusual. The subject of race injected itself in the Detroit Pistons locker room after a playoff loss to the Celtics. Dennis Rodman reportedly said that if Bird wasn't white he'd be considered "just another good guy," to which teammate Isiah Thomas chimed in his agreement.

Well, that caused a huge public backlash. Bird's reaction was not to be bothered at all by it. When it was clear the uproar wasn't going to subside quickly, Bird readily agreed to appear with Thomas at a press conference to help the Detroit star get off the hook and apologize about any misunderstanding.

Bird was also an extremely coachable player. When Jimmy Rodgers succeeded K.C. Jones as Celtics coach in 1988, Cousy said, "Jimmy knows that he won't have to worry about Bird. He's all set as far as he's concerned." Bird was adaptable to just about any coaching style.

In many ways he was another coach on the floor. He could also make some statements in the locker room that could only come from a fellow player. Such as the time he indicated that some of his teammates played like "sissies" in the blowout loss in Game 3 of the 1984 Finals. The Celtics won the next game and then the series in seven games. Coach Jones had to appreciate his candor and his ability as a motivator.

Bird loved to rile up opposing crowds in a good-natured fashion. The crowds on the road could often be hostile. He felt the '86 team played better when the crowd was totally against the Celtics. One night in 1986 during a Celtic visit to Sacramento that changed briefly. The NBA had recently put a franchise in the California state capital and the fans didn't yell obscenities at Bird or his Celtic teammates

"They weren't saying 'We love you Larry.' They were getting on me, but they enjoyed the game," he said. "You could tell. They weren't making remarks that were uncalled for, things that make you want to throw up."

The Celtics didn't play well in that game. It was the first game after the All-Star break and first game of the team's annual West Coast trip. Bird, a strong believer in practice, expected the Celtics to be off their game. "You can't take three, four or five days off, have one practice, and play the next night, and produce like you haven't missed anything. We're not that type of team. We've got guys that need to practice every day to keep their skills up, and I'm one of them."

The importance of practice is something Bird learned when he was in high school. Beezer Carnes, his best friend and teammate on the Spring Valley High squad, would arrive late or miss many of the team's shooting practices, which were held at 6 each morning.

"Our coach always told us he'd be the one to cost us a big game," Bird said. "And sure enough he missed three one-and-ones (from the foul line) when we had a six-point lead in the last minute of the game and we missed a chance to go to the state finals." His NBA statistics attest that Bird rarely missed from the free throw line, leading the league in four seasons. In the 1989-90 season, he made an astonishing 319 free throws out of 343 attempts.

Larry Joe Bird was not a great star in high school until his senior year, when he averaged more than 30 points per game at Spring Valley and was named to the All-State Team. Bird's hometown of French Lick, Indiana has a population of only a few thousand people, but the basketball gymnasium seated more than 2,000 and it was often filled for Bird's games. The movie *Hoosiers* illustrated the importance of basketball in Indiana.

Asked to give advice to any high school player with talent, he said, "I was blessed with good high school coaches. I always had somebody around to give me that extra push. I was out playing one day and my coach said, 'Boy you play a lot of basketball. You keep it up and one of these days it'll pay off for you. I'll give you one piece of advice. No matter how much you play, or how much time you put into it, or how many shots you take, there's always somebody down the road that puts in a little more.'"

Bird didn't think that was possible because he spent so much time practicing, but those words stuck with him for the rest of his career. It's hard to believe that a $2 million yearly salary was considered a lot of money for an NBA star in the 1980s. Now they're paying bench-warmers that much and giving even mid-level players much larger sums, thanks largely to the explosion of sports coverage on television and increasing fees paid to broadcast games.

Bird saw the emergence of big money in the NBA and predicted that it would prolong the careers of many players. "This life's too easy to turn down $2 million a year," he said. "You've got to be crazy. I don't say everybody stays in for the money, of course, they stay in for the love of the game, but the game's too easy. It's just nine months… That's why you'll see more superstars hanging around."

The Celtics' great vowed that he would never stay around as long as Boston's John Havlicek, who retired at 38. Yet, had back problems not forced his retirement at 35, Bird might have matched that mark. He just has a love of the game. And the basketball floor was a place in which he felt complete confidence, while off the floor he appeared at times somewhat awkward.

Off the court, Bird always was battling with his superstardom. Shy by nature, he had to learn to deal with the press and the fans. Some were puzzled when Bird said, "It's tough being Larry Bird."

He commented about what he meant by that statement. "Making two million dollars is the great part about it," he said. "The bad part about it is that it's demanding. People don't want to see the 11th or 12th man signing autographs. They want to see Larry Bird signing autographs. It gets monotonous at times. People are greedy just like everybody else. Everybody has their good days and their bad days, and celebrities and superstars and everybody else are the same. It's a pain sometimes, but sometimes it's a good feeling. I enjoy winning the championship, going home and being by myself or with my family, and talking about it."

Bird played a major role in bringing three championships to Boston. The '86 team has been ranked as one of the league's greatest ever. The team lost only one home game during the regular season, posting an impressive 67-15 record. The Celtics had their starting five and the "Green Team," which was another name for the club's second unit that entered the game and often increased the Boston lead. That's how good they were.

Watching Bird operate with the likes of Parish, McHale, Bill Walton, and company was a sight to behold. When Walton, who many believe was the greatest passing center of all time, combined with the greatest passing forward of all time it was like a beautifully choreographed dance.

While shy at times off the court, he didn't hesitate to voice his opinion if he believed an NBA ruling was unfair to his team. The Celtics failed to successfully defend their title against the Lakers in 1985 despite having home court advantage. The league had installed a new format that year calling for the first two games to be played in Boston, then three in Los Angeles, and the final two in Boston. The previous format is now only used for earlier playoff series, calling for two games at home, two away, then one at home, one away, and one at home.

"I prefer the 2-2-1-1-1 because I think the fifth game is very crucial in a seven-game series," Bird said. "Usually after the first four games it's 2-2 and I think the team that goes up 3-2 puts a lot of pressure on the other team because if you have one bad shooting night it's all over. That was the case last year, we came back for the sixth game and we didn't shoot well and the Lakers didn't shoot great, but they shot better than we did, and they were able to maintain a lead."

It is not surprising that Bird eventually found it dull playing golf all day in retirement and that he returned to the NBA as a head coach, a job he said he had no interest in when he retired. The move was a way to get back in the game. He couldn't play anymore, but being a coach could get those competitive juices flowing.

It's also not surprising that the Indiana Pacers had their best seasons when Bird was coach. He knows how to win and received instant respect upon his arrival in Indianapolis. Auerbach had seen Bird's ability to teach the game, making an instructional video with him. He is the only person to be named league MVP, Coach of the Year, and Executive of the Year. The coaching award came after he led the Pacers to a franchise best 58-24 record in the '97-'98 season. In his three years coaching Indiana, the Pacers reached the conference finals twice and the NBA finals in his final year there, where his quest for another ring was dashed by the Lakers.

The Celtics reached the mountaintop once more in 2008 and now are improving under young coach Brad Stevens to the point where they are close to being a championship team again. Top draft picks Jaylen Brown and Jayson Tatum, free agents Al Horford and Gordon Hayward, along with the acquisition of Kyrie Irving, have made the Celtics a viable title contender.

Bird reminds one of what someone said about Metro-Goldwyn-Mayer film producer Irving Thalberg: "As long as Irving lives, we are all great men." Unfortunately, Thalberg died at 37. Bird didn't die young, but his playing career ended about the same time. As each following year passed, Celtics fans realized how much they longed for those days. His mere presence made everybody better on the floor. As long as Bird was playing, no Celtics team could ever be bad.

Perhaps his longtime friend and archrival, the Lakers' Johnson, put it best when he told Bird, "You lied to me once. You said there will be another Larry Bird. There will never be another Larry Bird."

CHAPTER 3

JOHNNY MOST

Anyone who first listened to a Boston Celtics broadcast during the years that Johnny Most was the team's radio announcer could tell there was something different about the man doing the play-by-play. There had never been anybody quite like him, and there really never has been anybody comparable since.

From the time he began broadcasting Celtics games in 1953 to when he set down his microphone in 1990 due to ill health, Most portrayed his broadcasts as a clash of good against evil, with the Celtics always representing the cause of righteousness and goodness.

He tried to make the game as entertaining as he could, creating his own nicknames and vocabulary for players and situations. Most became a Boston institution, and when he died 25 years ago in 1993 at 69 there was a great sense of loss in the city. He would have had a lot of fun announcing the games of the current edition of the Celtics under Coach Brad Stevens.

Most was interviewed the morning after the Celtics had beaten the Philadelphia 76ers, 102-100, at Boston Garden to win the 1985 Eastern Conference finals, 4-1. Larry Bird made a key steal to ensure the victory.

3

Celtics' Broadcaster Was One Of A Kind

SAMMY COHEN, THE late sports editor of the *Boston Record-American* newspaper, once said of Johnny Most, "Most does not keep up with the play. What he does is, he broadcasts and the players try to keep up with him."

Most had a belief that telling listeners what is happening on the court is only part of the job. "I always considered this show business, as well as reporting" Most said. "You've got to entertain people for 2½ hours. And you've got to want them to listen to you. We've got to give them a reason why. So you created all these things around the game—the feuds, the fights, the nicknames. All that stuff. That's show business. Right in the middle is the actual ballgame. And if you're a fan you'll hear it. You put window dressing on it. You put flashy clothes on it."

He admitted that his broadcasts have a little professional wresting in them, while strongly adding the difference being "the actual event being legitimate, rather than fake."

Iavaroni and Bird are mixing it up, as Iavaroni put one on Bird, and Bird came right back at him. Now Malone wants Bird and Bird says, "Come on, let's go. Let's do it." Bird is talking to Malone. Well, Bird WANTS Malone. He wants him BADLY right now. And everybody is over there in front of Bird to keep him away.

Critics of Most's announcing style accused him of being the ultimate "homer" who watches the game through green-colored glasses.

He didn't dispute that his broadcasts were one-sided, but made no apologies.

"The approach I had initially was if I could convey a feeling of affection that it would help draw crowds," he said. "I learned to like these guys. I traveled with them all the time and learned to like them and just showed it, that's all. I said I'm not going to hold back because of the old-fashioned attitude of 'you've got to be strictly neutral.' I wasn't broadcasting everywhere. I was broadcasting to the Boston area. When you do a network broadcast you've got to respect that it's covering areas that don't particularly favor your team."

A classic example of Most's partiality was his description of Kevin McHale's hard foul on Laker forward Kurt Rambis during the fourth game of the 1984 NBA finals in Los Angeles. McHale appeared to nearly decapitate Rambis, using his arm to clothesline the Laker as he drove to the basket, clearing both benches.

Now it goes to Rambis, and Rambis is decked. Now he wants to charge (McHale)…Oh, you don't DARE touch him. You don't DARE. He was really decked by McHale and he didn't like it at all.

The Celtics ended up winning that crucial game in overtime to tie the series at two games apiece. The McHale foul seemed to have an impact on the momentum of the game turning toward Boston, the victory helping to erase the memory of an embarrassing lopsided loss in Game 3.

The Celtics have tied the series up. They laughed at them. They laughed at them. The papers were full of derision and mockery, but they came back and put it in everybody's faces.

Most had come to the Celtics from his native New York City, where he had been broadcasting New York Knicks games alongside colleague Marty Glickman, a former Olympic track athlete who had been a teammate of Jesse Owens. He also broadcast New York Giants football and Brooklyn Dodgers baseball games in the early '50s.

He made the move to Boston because the manager of the radio station where he worked wanted his son to replace Most on the Knicks' broadcasts. Team officials wanted the Most-Glickman combination to remain intact, but Most felt it was necessary to get out of an uncomfortable situation and tried out for the Celtics' job when it became available in 1953.

Curt Gowdy was the Celtics broadcaster at the time. He was gradually phasing himself out of the job because he was highly sought-after by the networks. Most won the job competition involving more than 30 applicants.

"It wound up with six finalists," Most said. "And each one of us was supposed to do two exhibition games. Each guy would do one until all six had done it and then you'd go around again. I was the sixth guy, and at the end of my stint Red (Auerbach) called (owner) Walter Brown and said, 'How do you like this guy?' And Walter said, 'Call off the rest of the auditions. This is it.' So we only went around once."

Most characterized the Celtics at that time as an entertaining team to watch. "They needed a big guy," he said. "They had a center who physically really wasn't a center, and that was Ed Macauley. He was 6-8 and weighed about 185 pounds. He had to go against guys like (Arnie) Risen and (George) Mikan. And they just blew him out of there physically. So he used to stay on the outside. He was a great shooter.

"They had all the other ingredients, including a great backcourt with (Bob) Cousy and (Bill) Sharman. They should have been attracting pretty good crowds but they weren't. They just couldn't get the ball off the boards. If they missed a shot, that was it. It was gone. There was no offensive rebounding at all, and frequently they lost their own rebounds on the other board."

Glickman had a great influence on his development as a broadcaster. During his tenure in New York, the Bronx-born Most also had an opportunity to work with legendary announcers Bill Stern and Ted Husing.

Most got the penchant for giving players nicknames from Glickman. "Marty was a master at that," he said. "He'd come up with things like 'Tricky Dick' for Dick Maguire, expressions like 'tricky dribbling' and also 'swish'—that was his." So Most borrowed from Glickman and developed his own nicknames and expressions.

He recalled a time when Glickman incorporated the name of a sponsor in his play-by-play. "There was a sponsor we had called Nedick's, which was a fast-food restaurant. Marty would say, 'The shot is good...like Nedicks.' When I came to Boston, Carling was one of our sponsors, and I used to say, "It's good...like Carling." Boston baseball fans might remember former Red Sox broadcaster Ken "Hawk" Harrelson using the same approach one season. As a home run was hit over the Green Monster. Harrelson would say, "Head for the Mountains," which happened to be the slogan of a beer sponsor.

Some of his most memorable nicknames given to opponents include: "The Hatchet Brothers" (Bobby Jones and Steve Mix), "McFilthy and McNasty" (Jeff Ruland and Ricky Mahorn), "Senator McVillain" (Tom McMillen) "Cry Kelly Cry" (Kelly Tripucka), and "The Beast of Broad Street" (Charles Barkley). Though he recognized early that Barkley was a great talent, he also believed he mouthed off too much, saying, "He needs to get a lip zipper."

When McHale came off the bench as a sixth man and usually made a solid contribution in the fourth quarter, Most referred to him as "Kevin the Fourth." John Havlicek was either the "Bouncing Buckeye from Ohio State" or "Jarrin' John." Dave Cowens was "Big Red" and 7-foot back-up center Hank Finkel was given the nickname "High Henry." Don Nelson was "Dynamite Don." Chris Ford, an excellent three-point shooter, was referred to as "Sir Longshot." When Dennis Johnson played for Phoenix he was "Mr. Nasty." After he was acquired by Boston in a trade he became simply "D.J."

Some other descriptive terms Most would use during a broadcast were "bang" (scoring on a jump shot), "pumpkin" (an easy shot close to the basket), "in the dip" (just before a player releases a free throw), "pulling a Stanislavski" (derived from the acting teacher when Most thought a player faked being fouled), "scoop" (an underhanded shot driving to the basket), "shot from the street" (a long shot), "stop and pop" (a pull-up jumper), and "rainbow" (high-arching shot).

When Most thought that a Celtics player was being manhandled by an opponent defensively, with the officials not calling a foul, he let his listeners know about it. For instance, when the New York Knicks' Bill Bradley was overly aggressive, he said that Bradley was a master of the "clutch-and-grab style defense." If a player was having an exceptional performance in all facets of the game, Most would say, "The only thing he hasn't done is sell popcorn."

He said that Stern gave him the flair for the dramatic.

Greer is going to put the ball into play. He gets it out deep and Havlicek steals it. Over to Sam Jones. Havlicek stole the ball. IT'S ALL OVER. IT'S ALL OVER. Johnny Havlicek is being mobbed by the fans. IT'S ALL OVER. Johnny Havlicek stole the ball. Oh boy, what a play by Havlicek at the end of this ballgame. A spectacular series comes to an end in spectacular fashion. John Havlicek is being hoisted aloft. He yells and raises his hands. Bill Russell wants to grab Havlicek. He hugs him. He squeezes John Havlicek. Havlicek saved this ballgame. Believe that. Johnny Havlicek saved this ballgame. The Celtics win it 110-109.

Most relished telling a story about Stern when he was broadcasting a college football game. "He was sitting over a public address system at the Cotton Bowl and the speaker was blaring so much that he couldn't hear. He had two guys lower his assistant over the side and they cut the cable to the public address system. And the guy never had any P.A. system that day because he cut it because he couldn't hear himself. Those were the days when guys like reporters and broadcasters were ribald. They really did whatever the hell they felt like doing to make that broadcast work."

Most called Husing the "absolute best ever" sports broadcaster. "Husing gave me the sly humor that sometimes I come up with," he said, "and the allegorical alliteration. I love that. Peter Piper picked a peck of pickled peppers. He was fabulous with that, absolutely fabulous."

The Celtics announcer enjoyed writing poetry since he was a young man. He announced one of his creations during a Celtics game against the Pistons. "I was getting angry at Kelly Tripucka and Bill Laimbeer, so I said, 'A garland of roses for Isaiah Thomas, and garlic and onions for Laimbeer and Tripucka.' "

He called himself a "young protégé of Husing's" as he began his broadcasting career. "I was just a young punk in my 20s and I got this opportunity to do all these great things," he said.

When Most arrived in Boston, he got his first piece of advice from the *Record-American's* Cohen, a legend himself in the city's media circles: "Keep doing everything you're doing, but just remember this is a big small town, and learn to love Boston." So he adjusted to Boston after growing up in a much larger city.

The *Record-American* later merged into what became known as today's tabloid-style *Boston Herald*, the competitor of *The Boston Globe*.

Most is a 1940 graduate of New York's DeWitt Clinton High School, which had an enrollment of as many as 12,000 students, making it what many believed to be the largest high school in the world at the time.

Dewitt Clinton has many other distinguished alumni, including actors Burt Lancaster, Larry Storch and Don Adams, screenwriter Paddy Chayefsky, playwright Neil Simon, as well as athletes such as middleweight boxing champion Sugar Ray Robinson, standout Yankees pitcher Eddie Lopat, and Dolph Schayes, the Syracuse Nationals' NBA star who is a member of the Naismith Memorial Basketball Hall of Fame.

"Robinson was supposed to be in my graduating class, but I don't think he bothered himself with such mundane things," Most said.

Recalling those days he said, "You have to remember it was a school that was all boys. So you can imagine what went on in those corridors." The school didn't become co-educational until 1983 and was the last school in the city to do so.

Most distinguished him himself as a bomber gunner in World War II, earning seven medals, and returned to earn a bachelor's degree in 1947 from Brooklyn College, where he played football and basketball.

After taking the Celtics job, Most soon learned to love the Hub and the team he broadcast. The Celtics of the early '50s featuring Bob Cousy, Sharman, and Macauley were fun to watch, but lacked that capable center, a void filled by Bill Russell in 1956. He provided the rebounding the team needed.

"They could execute," Most said. "They could run. It looked like a ballet, watching them. Cousy was a great, great, great player. He knew how to take advantage of everybody's skills. If you had a skill, he got the ball to you when it was time. It was a great club."

The Celtic announcer told many humorous stories about his days on the road with the team, although some were not so humorous at the time. Once he got into a fistfight instigated by St. Louis Hawks owner Ben Kerner. He asked then NBA Commissioner Maurice Podoloff to either fine Kerner or that he would take Kerner to court. Most said he believed Podoloff consented to his request. "I didn't want to take it to court, and the league didn't need that type of thing at the time anyway," he said. "It was still a struggling league."

He was harassed by fans at many NBA outposts, causing him to call Madison Square Garden "Madison Square Zoo" and Philadelphia the "City of Brotherly Hate."

Most enjoyed telling two stories about incidents that took place while he was broadcasting Boston games played in Philadelphia.

"I kept having a beef with a guy that used to sit behind me all season long," he said. "Now comes the playoffs. Howie McHugh, who was our beloved public relations man, used to sit with me a lot of times during the playoffs. So he's sitting with me and I said, 'Howie, this guy behind us, he can touch us—and he frequently does. He's obnoxious and he's got a big mouth, a nasty mouth. Don't let him get to you. He's going to call you names. He's going to call me names. He's going to call Boston names. He said OK, he would promise.

"Now Howie was more explosive than me, if that's possible. And this guy starts on us. And I said to myself, 'Gee, my friend sounds like he has a cold because he doesn't quite sound the same.' And Howie says, 'I can't stand it anymore. I cannot take it anymore. I'm going to clean this guy's clock. He turns around and it's the middleweight champion of the world, Joey Giardello. I said, 'Go ahead Howie. Rip 'im up.'"

He recalled another time at Convention Hall in Philadelphia when local fans were bothering him. Tom McNeeley, an Arlington native who had fought Floyd Patterson for the heavyweight championship, attended the game. He saw that Most was being harassed and walked over to sit next to him. "He had biceps, really big arms," Most said. "He put his arm around me and all of a sudden all the wise stuff, all of it, stopped. Nobody wanted anything to do with me as long as he was sitting there."

He always found it difficult to show his partiality when Coach

Billy Cunningham's '76ers faced the Celtics because of his warm relationship with Cunningham and his assistant Jack McMahon. He called Cunningham a "great guy" but a coach who has to be watched because "he'll do anything short of murder" to win. McMahon was the captain of a St. John's team that made the Final Four. Most had also broadcast St. John's basketball during his time in New York.

The Celtics-'76ers rivalry was fierce during much of Most's announcing tenure. It was also one where the '76ers were often accused of sour grapes. After a loss to the Celtics, the Sixers' Barkley said, "The Celtics know they cannot beat us." After losing a playoff series, some Philadelphia players were known to say "We still have the better team."

Most responded to that statement in this way: "I always say prove it. There's only one way to prove it. A team concept doesn't just mean talent. Talent is one of the major ingredients, of course. Stamina is one, determination is one, heart and character."

The '76ers franchise had originated in Syracuse where the team was named the Nationals, another heated rival of the Celtics. The rivalry continued when the Syracuse franchise moved to Philadelphia in 1963 after the Warriors, which had been Philadelphia's team, left for San Francisco the previous year.

Most once rented a house in the Boston area with some Celtic players and shared a room on the road with players such as Gene Conley, Tommy Heinsohn and Lou Tsioropoulos, a Lynn native and former University of Kentucky star, who backed up Heinsohn at forward while playing for Boston in the late '50s.

Conley, a fine athlete who passed away last year, also pitched for the Boston Braves and Red Sox in the '50 and '60s. During his playing career, he was considered by some to be two tacos short of a combination plate—in other words a bit crazy. "He may have been even crazier than me," Most said. He recalled a memorable time when the Celtics were in St. Louis. "(Conley) showed up for dinner with two six-packs of beer—TWO SIX-PACKS—because they only sold the low-alcohol (3.2) beer in St. Louis."

The 6-foot-8-inch Conley's most famous exploit was probably the time he left the team bus in 1962 with Red Sox teammate Pumpsie

Green in search of a restroom at a bar, only to find the bus gone upon returning. The bus, which had been stalled in New York traffic, left as soon as the gridlock eased. In a further twist, instead of rejoining the team like Green, Conley tried to board a plane to, of all places, Jerusalem.

Most likened the champion Celtics of the Bird era to the title teams Auerbach and Tommy Heinsohn coached because "they refuse to lose. They just don't like it." He believed it wasn't superior talent that was the main factor in Boston's victory over the Lakers in the 1984 championship series, but the Celtics' "superior character." In fact, he believed the Lakers had more talent than the Celtics that year.

The legendary broadcaster marveled at Larry Bird, not only because of his extraordinary skills, but because of his tough character. "Bird is the toughest guy on the club," he said. "He is as tough as they come. Mental toughness. He defies crowds. He deliberately gives quotes to the local newspapers to rile their crowd up. He did that in Cleveland. 'You want the Bird. You're going to get him. You're going to get the Bird.'"

He said his most depressing season was in '69-'70 after Russell and Sam Jones had retired. The announcer was "in shock" at how bad the team was after all those championship seasons. Russell had officially retired six weeks before the season and the club had to quickly find a coach. Heinsohn was selected, and he had his work cut out for him.

Five seasons later the Celtics were back on top of the basketball world. But the first few seasons after the last Russell title were challenging for Most as an announcer. "During the years we were terrible I used to find something I could hang my hat on, like a ray of hope," he said. "Like when Rick Robey came in we were a terrible team. He was one of the hopes for the future at the time. He replaced Cowens as the starting center. Cowens worked very hard with him and started to develop him in his own image."

His greatest professional disappointment was that he was never given an opportunity to broadcast on a network. He was told by one network executive that his physical appearance wouldn't appeal to female fans. "I said, 'Doesn't knowledge, or personality, or sense of humor count anymore?' He said, 'No.' That's why with so many of the guys you say, 'How the fuck did he get that job?' That's still a sore spot with me. But you live with it. You don't quit because of that."

Most would have left the Celtics only for a network offer or an NBA general manager's job. He almost did become a general manager when the Chicago Zephirs approached him about taking that job in the early '60s. But the team was sold and moved to Baltimore, where it became the Bullets, and the new owners wanted a general manager with local connections.

Even though he technically didn't broadcast on a national network, he did get some of the same feeling when the Celtics were broadcast for 12 seasons on WBZ, which has a 50,000 watt clear-channel radio signal that can be heard in 38 states. The station is included in the ratings of 11 states.

"People heard the broadcasts in Milwaukee and Chicago," he said. "There are only about six stations in the country that have that type of signal, like WCAU in Philly and KDKA in Pittsburgh," he said. "Having the games on WBZ was just like being on a network."

As a result of that, fans sometimes would approach Most before road games. "I had people come up to me and say, 'I'm a New York Knicks fan. I always have been, but I really appreciate the way you broadcast. It's very entertaining. I like it even though I hate you sometimes.' When they said things like that it was very gratifying. I like being an announcer who stirs strong reactions."

Not only was Most's style unique, so was his voice, which was very distinctive. His long history of smoking likely contributed to the sound that came out of his mouth, a gravelly growl unlike any other announcer's voice.

Most once taught a course in broadcasting at Cambridge School of Broadcasting, which later became Graham Junior College. One of his pupils was Gary LaPierre, who would become a morning fixture on WBZ radio for many years. Tom Cheeks, who announced Toronto Blue Jays games, was also one of his students. Yet Most couldn't recall anybody who reminded him stylistically of himself.

The Naismith Basketball Hall of Fame's trustees voted to give Most an award named after the man he replaced. It is called the Curt

Gowdy Media Award and was given to Most shortly after his retirement for his contribution to the game as a broadcaster.

He truly was one of kind. One of his signature lines was "This is Johnny Most, high above courtside." If there's a game going on Heaven, Johnny is probably broadcasting it.

CHAPTER 4

ROCKY MARCIANO

The genesis of this chapter is related to a story I heard about Richard "Dino" Colombo being a friend of the late heavyweight boxing champion Rocky Marciano. I knew Dino well because he was the friend of my late uncle Joe Daly and also a neighbor in Gardner, Massachusetts.

Eventually I arranged an interview with Dino and asked him to talk about his recollections of Rocky. Well, it turned out not only had he been a close friend of Rocky, he had grown up in the same Brockton, Massachusetts neighborhood and was an occasional sparring and running partner.

The Colombo and Marciano families remain close, and Dino is also related to Rocky by marriage. Dino passed away in 2014, so I am glad he shared his memories of Rocky with me. A physical therapist by trade, his chief hobby was being a sculptor, making his creations in his home's basement workshop.

His sculpture depicting "The Brockton Blockbuster" can be found in a Brockton cafe near where he once lived. I visited that cafe, as well as Rocky's boyhood neighborhood in 2010, and talked to some people there as well. Next year will mark the 50th anniversary of Marciano's death in a plane crash.

4

"He Beat Them All Because He Refused To Lose"

STANDING BEHIND A baseball backstop in the Ward 2 section of Brockton, Massachusetts—across the street from his boyhood home—is a stone marker dedicated to Brockton's favorite son, Rocky Marciano. On the marker is an inscription that reads: Rocky Marciano, 1923-1969, the Brockton Blockbuster, Undefeated Heavyweight Champion of the World, 49-0, September 23, 1952 to April 28, 1956.

Also are the words: He Beat Them All Because He Refused to Lose.

The marker stands at James Edgar Playground, the place where the young Rocky played countless hours of baseball, basketball, football, and just about any other sport he could get involved in. He played them all, including hockey, but it wasn't one of the traditional sports youngsters engage in that would gain him the most notoriety.

During his life he was famous in a way he could have only imagined. Holding the heavyweight boxing championship during Rocky's time was a very big deal in America, while today people often scratch their heads when trying to come up with the name of today's heavyweight champion.

A few youngsters playing basketball today on the same court on which he played know that Rocky was heavyweight champion, but little more than that. A teenager offered that he heard Rocky's lucky number was 13, which, if true, is interesting in that it was in Round 13 that he knocked out Jersey Joe Walcott to win the title.

They point to the house located only a few steps away where Rocky lived on Dover Street. It is a modest yellow two-story house with a marker on it designating its importance in the Marciano story. These boys can give you few details of his life. It isn't a subject taught in Brockton's schools. They told me I should stop by Petti's Market for more facts about Rocky during his Brockton days. Rocky's family had moved to Dover Street when he was a young boy from nearby Brook Street, where Rocky was born Rocco Francis Marchegiano on September 1, 1923. That house also still stands.

Petti's Market is located just down the road at the corner of Brook and Belmont streets. It was at 80 Brook Street that Rocky spent his early boyhood years, living on the second floor of a house owned by his grandparents. Todd Petti, who works for the Massachusetts Lottery Commission, is one of the keepers of the Marciano flame. Boxing memorabilia related to Brockton's favorite son can be found in one of the storefront windows.

Mr. Petti is the grandson of the founder of Petti's Market, which celebrated its 100th anniversary in 2013. His father, Charlie Petti, met Rocky several times. "Rocky was seven years older than my father," he said. "Everybody remembers him as being a great athlete. Everybody looked up to Rocky." Todd occasionally pitches in to help other members of his family run the store today. Those wishing to know more about Rocky are given a handout with a brief biography of the champion written by Charlie Petti.

Todd was happy to bring me across the street to George's Cafe. The Petti Market storefront tribute to Rocky can simply be called an appetizer compared to what awaits you at the cafe, a Brockton landmark for more than 75 years. Wall after wall is decorated with photos, boxing gloves, and other memorabilia dedicated to The Brockton Blockbuster, as well as former middleweight champion Marvin Hagler, who wasn't born here, but trained in Brockton under the Petronelli brothers. George's has always been owned by the Tartaglia family and is now owned by Charlie Tartaglia. One of his uncles was a corner man for Rocky in many of his early bouts in Providence, Rhode Island.

Muhammad Ali, who fought Marciano in a computer generated

"Super Fight" shortly before Rocky's death, visited the cafe on two occasions. Originally, Marciano didn't like Ali, but that changed during the filming of the Super Fight, when a mutual friend, trainer Angelo Dundee, encouraged Marciano to get to know Ali, who always referred to Marciano as "champ" during the filming of the fight, which ended up looking remarkably realistic. Marciano, who was balding, wore a toupee and trained to restore his fighting weight so that he could look as close as possible to way he did when he was champion.

Dundee would later say that Marciano told him that he had changed his mind about Ali after being critical of the "Louisville Lip" early in Ali's career. Interestingly, Ali, who was always known for his braggadocio, never said that he definitely would have beaten Marciano if they had been contemporaries. Ali told Howard Cosell that his arms hurt after the staged the computer fight from the punches of Marciano, who was in his 40s at the time. "He hit so hard it rattled my kinfolk in Africa," Ali said.

Rocky died before he knew the outcome of the Super Fight, which was shown in theaters in 1970. Neither fighter knew the result when they were staging the fight, as several endings were filmed. The computer's verdict: Marciano over Ali in a knockout in the 13th round. Maybe 13 *was* Rocky's lucky number.

Ali told Cosell that he believed that Marciano was better than Joe Frazier, who defeated Ali in his comeback fight and lost to Ali in two epic rematches. Cosell told Ali that he got more humble when the discussion turned to Marciano. Ali regarded Marciano as a brawler, instead of a scientific fighter, yet he had great respect for him, especially after the Super Fight filming. "I don't know if I would have beaten him in his heyday," Ali said. "In his heyday, he may have won." One can't remember the usually confident Ali talking about another fighter in the same way.

In a 1966 Australian television interview, Marciano was asked about his assessment of the champion, then known as Cassius Clay. "I don't know how good he is," Marciano said. "He hasn't been hit directly in the chin. His talent is getting away from a punch. In all of Clay's fights he's never been outstanding...It's going to take a good opponent to show how good he is." He acknowledged though that he thought that Clay resembled Joe Lewis physically and had the ability close to that of the Brown Bomber, ability that could possibly lead him to boxing greatness.

Later in the interview, he made it clear that Clay's promotions of his Muslim religion and draft evasion did not sit well with him. "At first he was good for boxing, predicting the round he'd win and all that," he said. "He brought a lot of new people into boxing. He overdid it. He talked too much. When he brought religion into the picture the last two years, he's been bad for boxing."

Just a few steps from Petti's Market is the boyhood home of Richard "Dino" Colombo, who later moved to Gardner, Massachusetts after college to work as a physical therapist. Though five years younger than Rocky, they became friends, growing up in the same Brockton neighborhood. While doing his road work, Rocky would stop by Dino's house and say, "Hey Dino, you want to take a walk?"

They would often run also, sometimes ending up as far as the area known as the Blue Hills in Milton, located 10 miles from Boston. Brockton is about 24 miles south of the Hub. At times they would run around the Edgar playground. "He loved having somebody he knew to run with," Dino said. When Rocky became more and more well known, Dino said people would honk their horns as they passed them. Some put a cool towel around his neck.

Dino, who was a star football center at Brockton High and later at Boston University, spent many hours at the Brockton YMCA during his schoolboy years. Rocky also spent a lot of time there. "I'd be playing basketball and somebody would say, 'Rocky's looking for you.' I'd go and spar with him," Dino said.

Not only was Dino close to Rocky, but his family and Rocky's were very close. In fact, Dino's father Michelangelo was the best friend of Rocky's father, Pierino, who labored for many years in a Brockton shoe factory. "My parents and Rocky's parents would sometimes go out together," Dino said.

He remembers Rocky's mother, Pasqualina, and father as having quite different constitutions. "His mother was as strong as a bull and smart and sweet, while his father was more ill and sickly," he said. Both were Italian immigrants.

People thought that Rocky's strength came from him mother's side. Dino believed that Pierino's service in World War I contributed to his frail constitution, particularly the poison gas that was used during that war. "He inhaled some stuff and his health went downhill after that," he said.

Dino was not the only one of the next generation to have strong ties with the Marchegianos, which is Rocky's true last name. "The kids of both families were very close," he said. "My brother Armond married Rocky's sister Betty. We were like one big family." Dino recalled that when Rocky came to that wedding, Rocky's manager Al Weil said, "You are here to see the next heavyweight champion of the world." Dino said "everybody went crazy" upon hearing that.

He remembers proudly when he was at the Italian American Club with Rocky in Boston and Rocky announced, "This is my assistant, Dino Colombo." Dino is also a talented sculptor. His sculpture of Rocky is prominently displayed behind the bar at George's Café. When your father is named Michelangelo maybe you are destined to have some artistic talent.

Yet there was another Colombo from the old neighborhood, not related to Dino, who would have a much greater impact on Rocky's career. Alisay "Allie" Colombo, who lived next door to Rocky, saw him right after he got home from serving in World War II and encouraged him to pursue a professional boxing career. Rocky had gotten his first real taste of boxing competition when he was asked to fight in an armed forces tournament, which he won in 1946. He also had distinguished himself in the Gold Gloves Championship. He missed out on going to the Olympics when he hurt his hand and could no longer compete for a spot.

Baseball had always been Rocky's first love. He had been a catcher, but he failed to catch on with the Chicago Cubs at a tryout camp in North Carolina. He then realized that boxing was his best chance to succeed in professional sports.

He had left Brockton High in 1940 after his sophomore year so that he could get a job to help out his family. He wore the number 1 on his football uniform, which turned out to be prophetic.

Though he loved and respected his father, he didn't want to spend the rest of his life working in a factory. His father encouraged him to make something of himself. One could say that Rocky's determination to avoid his father's fate was a major motivator in making Rocky what he became.

Allie Colombo offered to do whatever he could to help Rocky achieve boxing success, and the two men became a team. Allie wrote about Rocky to Al Weil, a well-known fight manager in New York. Dino Colombo recalled that Allie and Rocky bought an old car that barely ran to make some of the excursions to train under Charlie Goldman after Weil agreed to manage Marciano. Prior to that, they would hitch a ride on a truck heading for New York.

When Goldman first saw Rocky fight, he quickly realized Marciano was a terrific puncher, but had no real concept of footwork and boxing style. Many boxing people had discouraged Rocky about his boxing future because of his style and physical attributes. He was just over 5 feet, 10-inches and weighed 183 pounds. Besides, he had short arms, with a 67-inch wingspan that seemed woefully inadequate. Some told him pursuing a career in boxing was a waste of time.

The one thing that was impossible to measure was Rocky's heart and determination. If they had been able to measure those, they would have found them to be off the charts. Rocky was ready to learn how to minimize his deficiencies and maximize his strengths.

His brother-in-law Armond, who was a highly successful football coach at Brockton High, gave Rocky a high tribute when he said, "If I had eleven football players with the courage, determination, and desire of Rocky Marciano, I would never lose a football game."

Perhaps his biggest problem, his reach, was solved when Goldman suggested he crouch more, making him harder to hit and allowing him to pummel his opponents from the inside. Goldman did nothing to change Marciano's powerhouse overhand right, which Marciano referred to as his "Suzy-Q." Marciano knew he had to use a specific tactic to be effective. "I had to come up from underneath," he said. "I couldn't jab with the great jabbers."

He became known as someone who trained hard for his fights, once saying, "I have always adhered to two principles. The first one is to train hard and get in the best possible physical condition. The second is to forget about the other fellow until you face him in the ring and the bell sounds for the fight."

As Marciano began his professional career, Weil suggested a name change because both fight announcers and the press were having a problem pronouncing Marchegiano and spelling it. Rocky had once fought under the name of Rocky Mack and Weil suggested that might be a solution. But Marciano was proud of his Italian heritage, opting instead to condense his name from Marchegiano to a more manageable Marciano.

Many of Marciano's early professional fights were held in Providence, where he developed a large following, especially in the city's Italian-American community. "A bunch of us would go down from Brockton to Providence to watch his fights," recalled Dino Colombo. "He had a cheering section from the old neighborhood." Of his 49 professional fights, 29 were held in Providence.

Two of those bouts were against a little-known fighter named "Tiger" Ted Lowry, who gave Rocky trouble on both occasions. The two met in October of 1949, with Rocky winning a unanimous 10-round decision. It was the same outcome a year later. For some reason, Lowry was a tough opponent for him.

One could say that Marciano's "coming out party" was when he knocked out highly regarded Rex Lane in the sixth round of a nationally televised fight in July of 1951. His next fight marked Marciano's only professional bout held in Boston, as he knocked out Freddie Beshore in the fourth round.

Then he defeated one of one of his boyhood idols, Joe Louis, who had come out of retirement and was attempting to regain the title after holding it for 12 years. Marciano was emotional after the eighth-round knockout of Louis, which basically ended Louis' comeback bid. He visited the "Brown Bomber" in his locker room after the fight with tears in his eyes. He told the press, "The man was a true champion. I didn't enjoy what I did tonight. Ten years ago it might have gone the other way."

Then, after posting a second-round knockout of Harry "Kid" Matthews a year later he was ready for his title shot against the champion Walcott.

The fight, which was held outdoors in Philadelphia, generated a great deal of interest in the sports world. Marciano had begun his professional boxing journey in 1947 with a knockout of a fighter named Lee Eperson in Holyoke, Massachusetts. Now just five years and 42 victories without a loss later, he was in a position to win the heavyweight championship.

Interestingly, there was another piece of history being made that night of September 23, 1952. It was the first heavyweight championship bout televised via a "pay per view" set-up. The fight was sent coast-to-coast, appearing in 49 theaters in 31 cities.

Some of the members of Rocky's family were on hand at ringside, as well as some friends, while others watched via closed circuit. But for those left back in Brockton, finding out what happened in the fight was more difficult because the only radio broadcast they could receive was in Spanish. As was usually the case during a Marciano fight at this time, Brockton's Main Street was shut down and people gathered near the building housing the local newspaper, *The Brockton Enterprise*.

Those uninterested in the fight may have been watching Richard Nixon's famous "Checkers" speech being broadcast that night.

Walcott stunned Marciano in the first round by sending him to canvas, marking the first time Rocky had ever been knocked down. That got Rocky's attention immediately. Walcott didn't knock him down again, but it was clear the champion was leading on points heading into the 13th round. It was in the early part of that round when Marciano backed Walcott into the ropes and delivered what has been called one of the most devastating punches in boxing history. "I didn't know what hit me," Walcott said after the fight.

Rocky had shown throughout his career to be a true gentleman and sportsman. He said of Walcott, "He proved to me what a champion is made of. I only hope I can be as good as him."

Walcott was equally gracious, saying Marciano was the best fighter he ever fought, adding that he was "happy to lose to such a gentleman."

Marciano met Walcott again in a rematch in Chicago eight months later. This time, Rocky finished Walcott early, knocking him out in just the first round. Roland LaStarza, whom Marciano had beaten in a decision in 1950, was his next opponent. LaStarza had said he believed that he should have won that decision and planned to take care of Rocky the next time. Marciano made it clear who the better fighter was in the rematch, dominating the bout and scoring a technical knockout in the 11th round.

His boxing career almost ended in 1949 when he met Carmine Vingo in a fight prior to the first LaStarza bout. Rocky had knocked out Vingo in the sixth round, leaving his opponent unconscious. Vingo was brought to the hospital and remained that way for some time. Rocky vowed that he would quit boxing if Vingo died. He visited the hospital and prayed for his recovery. Vingo needed brain surgery, but did regain consciousness. He spent two months in the hospital before being released. The fighter was partially paralyzed for the rest of his life. Vingo and Marciano became lifelong friends.

He successfully defended his title in consecutive hard-fought victories against former heavyweight champion Ezzard Charles in his only two fights of 1954. That was followed by a knockout of British champion Don Cockell in San Francisco the next year..

His final fight was a ninth-round knockout of Archie Moore. Moore, a longtime light heavyweight champion, was a talented fighter and hard puncher. The challenger trained for the fight in Massachusetts in the Berkshire County city of North Adams at Camp Kenwood.

More than 60,000 showed up for the fight at Yankee Stadium on September 21, 1955, while millions either watched it on closed-circuit television or listened on radio. Moore stunned Marciano with a right hand in the second round that sent him to the canvas for the second and last time in his career. As in the first Walcott fight, Rocky recovered to knock out Moore, this time ending the fight in the ninth round.

At 32, Marciano decided he had enough of the fight game, retiring on April 27, 1956 as the only undefeated heavyweight champion. When asked during a press conference if he might consider returning to the ring in the future, he said, "If Joe Louis couldn't do it, then I will not attempt to."

Marciano told reporters that he had promised his wife, Barbara, on a vacation trip to South America that he would retire from the ring. The former Barbara Cousens, six years his junior, had married Rocky in 1950. They had met at a dance in Brockton.

What he didn't disclose at the press conference was another reason he had decided to retire. According to late boxing insider Burt Randolph Sugar, Rocky had hurt his back while playfully tossing his baby daughter Mary Ann in the air. Doctors advised him not to fight anymore because he risked aggravating the injury, which might make it difficult for him to walk normally. He remains the only undefeated heavyweight champion in history.

Three years after retiring, Marciano later flirted briefly with the idea of a comeback when Sweden's Ingemar Johansson became champion by beating Floyd Patterson. He actually trained for about a month before deciding to remain retired. One of New York's great sportswriters, Jimmy Cannon, was a friend of Marciano's. In his column, he advised Rocky against making a comeback. Of his decision to stay retired, Marciano said, "I didn't have the same feeling, the same hunger. I couldn't concentrate on boxing the way I once did."

Rocky led a comfortable life in retirement, acting as an advertising spokesman for some companies and also becoming involved in other business ventures. He was constantly in demand to speak. It was on his way to a speaking engagement in Des Moines, Iowa on August 31, 1969 that Marciano died in a plane crash.

The pilot, Glen Belz, and Frank Ferrell were also killed in the crash. Both men were from Des Moines and had flown to Chicago to pick up Marciano. Ferrell had known Rocky since his boyhood. Marciano agreed to make a speech in Des Moines before returning to his home in Florida, where a birthday celebration was planned for the next day.

The Cessna single-engine plane hit a tree and crashed less than two miles short of the runway of a small airport in Newton, Iowa on an overcast night. Belz had not radioed that he was experiencing any trouble. Mrs. Floyd Schwartz, a neighbor living close to crash site, reported that she heard the plane's engine "sputter, stop, sputter again, and then quit" before the crash.

Rocky and Barbara had adopted a son, Rocky Jr., just a few

months before his death. Upon hearing the tragic news, Rocky's mother spoke emotionally in Italian with words that translated to, "My son, the heart of my life."

Hundreds turned out for Rocky's funeral, including Joe Louis, who said, "God got the best when he took Rocky Marciano."

His friend Allie Colombo had died just eight months earlier in a freak truck accident that had taken place in a supermarket warehouse. Together, they created a moment in time that Brockton and the world will never forget.

Partly through the efforts of the Petti family and other Marciano fans, the World Boxing Council provided funding for a statue of Rocky, which was unveiled in Brockton on Sunday, September 23, 2012, marking the 60th anniversary of Marciano's victory over Walcott and just a few weeks after what would have been his 89th birthday.

For awhile, it appeared that the construction of the statue might be in jeopardy. The WBC had pledged to provide the funds for it and commissioned a sculptor to make a small model of its design, which sat in the Petti's Market storefront. But for a few years nothing happened to make the statue a reality. Finally, WBC President Jose Sulaiman gave the go-ahead to release the funding to create the statue, which was designed by sculptors Mario Rendon and Victor Gutierrez.

Sulaiman also granted Brockton's request that it be placed in his hometown. It stands outside Rocky Marciano Stadium, where the high school football team, nicknamed the Boxers, plays its games.

Peter Marciano idolized his famous brother, who was several years older. At the unveiling ceremony, he said, "It's finally here. It's something you can look at. It's something you can touch and you really believe it."

Brockton Mayor Linda Balzotti gazed at the statue and said, "It's so nice to have you back where you belong."

Rocky Marciano stands as an inspiration and example of what determination and a dream can produce.

CHAPTER 5

CARL YASTRZEMSKI

He appears at Fenway Park rarely now, usually when a special event is being held on the field to recognize a ballplayer. His hair has turned white, reflecting the fact he's in his late 70s. His number 8 appears on the right field deck façade among the 10 retired numbers in Red Sox history. When he said goodbye as a player in 1983, fans knew it was the end of an era in Red Sox history.

Although he has been retired for more than three decades, there are still plenty of fans today who can think back to watching Carl Yastrzemski play. It had been Yastrzemski who put the Red Sox back on the baseball map after many losing seasons, winning the Triple Crown in Boston's "Impossible Dream" pennant-winning season of 1967.

The Boston franchise has been on the upswing ever since. After not reaching the 1 million attendance mark in the six seasons prior to '67, the Sox drew more than 1.7 million that year and haven't been below a million since. Boston reached the 3 million mark for the first time in 2008. The Red Sox honored the '67 team during the 2017 season on its 50th anniversary, bringing back many players from that special group to give them another chance to take a bow.

Yaz holds the team record in seasons played (23), games (3,308), runs (1,816), hits (3,419), doubles (646), runs batted in (1,844), extra base hits (1,157), and total bases (5,539). The 18-time All-Star led the American League in hitting three times and won seven Gold Gloves. "Yaz," as he is often called, was elected to the Baseball Hall of Fame in 1989 in his first year of eligibility.

The following story, slightly revised, appeared in the *Fitchburg-Leominster Sentinel & Enterprise* on October 4, 1983. It chronicled my time at Fenway Park during his last day in baseball.

5

The Man Emerges
At Long Last

THE REPORTER FROM Fitchburg had been waiting for more than an hour Sunday to meet the man—the man they call Yaz.

He had begun his wait at noon in the Red Sox clubhouse, two hours before Boston's scheduled game with the Cleveland Indians, the 162nd of what had been a disappointing season for the local entry in the American League East.

Spring training hopes had been dashed by July, but nobody was thinking about that now. People were thinking about the historical significance of the game, marking the end of an illustrious career.

When the reporter stepped into Boston clubhouse, he felt that this is one of the fringe benefits of being a newspaperman, entering the players' inner sanctum that few fans ever get a chance to see. It was the beginning of many thrills for him on this day, a day he will never forget.

He had come at noon because he wanted ample time to perform several tasks: meet Yastrzemski and give him the page dedicated to him in Saturday's *Sentinel & Enterprise*, one the reporter had compiled; and also ask him to sign a wonderful full-page photograph of Yaz he had ripped out of the 1972 Red Sox yearbook.

A player that the reporter wanted to seek out for an interview was Wade Boggs, the second-year Boston third baseman who was celebrating his first American League batting title with a .361 average, the highest Sox mark since Ted Williams hit .388 in 1957. A feature story was in order about the man who seemed to be the heir-apparent to the Yastrzemski legend.

With Yastrzemski nowhere in sight, the reporter found Boggs, introduced himself, and asked for the interview. Could I meet him in the dugout at 12:45? Sure thing.

Wondering what to do next, the reporter caught a glimpse of manager Ralph Houk, also known as "The Major" for his World War II exploits, sitting at his office desk. The reporter walked in, introduced himself again, told him of the Boggs feature, and asked him to compare Boggs and Yastrzemski at a similar age. He talked for about 10 minutes. The reporter thanked him and left. Still about 20 minutes before the Boggs interview. The reporter approached Walt Hriniak, the Red Sox batting instructor, and asked him to compare the two men's attitude toward the game. More quotes for the notebook.

Time for the reporter to approach one of his favorite players, part-time center fielder Rick Miller, who has been handing out what looks like some type of All-Star ballot to all the players. He wanted to know whether Miller remembered a hit that he considered one of the more important safeties of the 1975 pennant-winning season.

"Rick, I'm Chris Daly of the *Fitchburg-Leominster Sentinel & Enterprise*. Fitchburg is about 50 miles west...He cut in, 'Yes, I know where Fitchburg is.'"

The reporter continued, "I wonder if you remember one of your hits that I thought was so important to the success of the '75 team. It was a game in July at Shea Stadium against the Yankees. You hit a single up the middle off "Catfish" Hunter that scored the game's only run. Miller nodded his head approvingly, saying, "Yes, I remember."

It's funny how moments stay in your memory. That was the same game that Fred Lynn made an athletic diving catch in left centerfield off Craig Nettles, preventing a triple and a possible victory by the Yankees, who were trying to stay in the pennant race. They were playing at Shea while Yankee Stadium was being renovated.

The Red Sox won both ends of a doubleheader that day, with Bill Lee besting Hunter in the opener, and Roger Moret tossing his only shutout of the season in the nightcap as Boston won more comfortably, 6-0. It was the first time the Yankees had suffered a shutout sweep of a doubleheader since 1958.

After saying goodbye to Miller, Boggs beckoned to the reporter that he was ready to talk. He followed the third baseman down the tunnel underneath the stands where all the Red Sox players travel to the dugout. At the end of the tunnel was the green of Fenway Park, a park that Red Sox historian George Higgins, in an entertaining volume called *The Ultimate Baseball Book*, wrote "assaults your senses" upon entering it. The book also contains Higgins' comment, "Like Heaven, Fenway Park is difficult to get into."

The amazing thing to the reporter was that Boggs was not getting more attention from the press. Perhaps, because it was Yastrzemski's final game, the media hadn't really noticed much that he was completing a fabulous year. The reporter wasn't complaining. For approximately 25 minutes, he and Wade Boggs—Wade Boggs the American League batting champion—sat together in the dugout talking about hitting and his career with the Red Sox.

The interview concluded, Boggs was thanked and the reporter walked back down the tunnel and returned to the clubhouse to look for Yastrzemski, who was still not visible. He decided to stand around for a few minutes. It wasn't long before he heard a familiar voice directly behind him, saying, "Does anybody know what's going on around here?"

He turned to find a half-dressed Yastrzemski moving toward his locker. The reporter introduced himself and he quickly responded, "How ya doing?," barely breaking stride. This seemed to be a reflex action caused by years of dodging press people.

He followed him to his locker and said, "I know you've been besieged by the media, and don't worry, I'm not going to try to interview you. I'd like to give you something." He was handed the *Sentinel & Enterprise's* tribute to him and Yastrzemski said thanks. He also graciously signed the photograph.

Included in the envelope containing the newspaper page was a brief letter to Yastrzemski from Chris Daly, the longtime fan, not the reporter. The fan wrote that he had been particularly struck by a quote in a Boston newspaper, where he said, "Since 1967, I have gone into what I consider a shell."

The fan wrote that it reminded him of a passage about the Sox slugger written by Roger Angell, the best baseball writer in America. Writing in his book, *The Summer Game,* about his observation of Yastrzemski in the clubhouse following the pennant-winning victory over the Twins in 1967, Angell commented:

"There was something sad here—perhaps the thought that for Yastrzemski, more than for anyone else, this summer could not come again. He had become a famous star, with all the prizes and ugly burdens we force on the victims of celebrity, and from now on he would be set apart from us and his teammates and the easy time of his youth."

Yastrzemski's gesture of running around the perimeter of the field on Saturday and Sunday, slapping fans' hands along the way in a "high five" to thank them, was an indication that, fittingly, he had come out of his shell. As the eloquent *Boston Globe* columnist Leigh Montville wrote, "The man had emerged."

This was his final gift to the fans of Boston. Since 1967, that incredible year when people thought he could walk on water, he had partially shielded himself from outsiders. But now, during his final shining moment, he gave something the fans had wanted—himself. "I wanted to show my emotions," he told reporters.

The Boston standout had come a long way since his boyhood days on a potato farm on New York's Long Island, playing sandlot baseball and also excelling at basketball, a sport for which he won a scholarship to Notre Dame. He stayed in South Bend one year before signing with the Red Sox in 1959.

Babe Ruth once commented that baseball is not a game one can pick up late in adolescence and expect to be good. "The only real game in the world I think is baseball," he said. "You've got to start from way down, at the bottom, when you're 6 or 7 years old. You can't wait until you're 15 or 16. You've got to let it grow up with you, and if you're successful and you try hard enough, you're bound to come out on top, just like these boys have come out on top now."

Casey Stengel had an accolade for only his best players. The "Old Perfessor" would say, "You done splendid." Better words could not be used to describe Yastrzemski's career as a Red Sox player. Yaz's hard work, dedication, and love of the game ensured that he would come out on top. He was the consummate professional.

Thanks for the memories.

CHAPTER 6

WADE BOGGS

Wade Boggs celebrated his first American League batting title on October 3, 1983, the final game of Boston's season. Yet few reporters were paying attention to him because that day happened to be Carl Yastrzemski's final day in a Red Sox uniform. Boggs would have won his first batting title the previous year, but he didn't have enough plate appearances to qualify.

After Carney Lansford was injured that year, Boggs took over at third base and never looked back. He played so well the Sox traded Lansford to Oakland in the off-season. The job then belonged to Boggs and he took advantage of it. So on "Yaz"'s memorable day, Boggs sat in the Red Sox dugout prior to the game, quietly savoring his achievement, and talking about his young career and the departure of the captain.

Others were also helpful in providing insight about Boggs, including manager Ralph Houk, scout Eddie Popowski, and hitting coach Walt Hriniak. Boggs went on to a Hall of Fame career that included 12 All-Star appearances, five American League batting titles, two Gold Gloves, and the elusive World Championship in 1996 as a member of the New York Yankees.

It was a pleasure to be in attendance 33 years after that dugout meeting when the Red Sox retired Boggs' number 26 in 2016, taking its rightful place on the right field deck façade with those of other team legends.

6

"Chicken Man" Ruled Roost At Fenway

WADE BOGGS SPENT six seasons in the minor leagues before getting his shot in the Majors, the last five of those seasons hitting over .300. Was Boggs frustrated that it took so long for the parent club to call him up? "No," he said. "I was young. I started playing when I was 18 and joined the Red Sox when I was 23. I give my best every day, whether I'm playing for (Pawtucket Red Sox manager) Joe Morgan) or Ralph Houk."

He believes his experience in the International League at Pawtucket, which he called "the toughest pitchers' league in the minor leagues," gave him invaluable training for The Show. Boggs disagreed with some who called the American League a "hitters' league." Such judgments were made after the league didn't have a 20-game winner in 1982.

"We have several guys who have won 20 this year ('83) like Ron Guidry and (Lamarr) Hoyt, " he said. "There aren't many Astro-turf fields in this league. There are a lot of hits with Astro-turf."

The Red Sox third baseman never was close to Carl Yastrzemski personally, which is something probably many of his teammates could identify with. "Yaz" was never close to many of his teammates, perhaps because he had seen so many come and go that he didn't want to undergo the emotional toll of watching a teammate be traded, retire, or be cut from the team. Talking about his departing captain, Boggs said, "He's basically an independent person, as are a lot people in this game. He helped me last year when I wasn't playing. We'd talk about various pitchers. It made it a lot easier to face them."

He celebrated his first batting title with a .361 average in his first full season in The Show. It took Yastrzemski three years to win his first batting title, taking the crown with a .321 average in 1963. Yet Yaz was 24 when he won his first title, one year younger than Boggs.

Boggs admired Yastrzemski's determination to be successful. "He'd always take extra batting practice and work on the extra things to put you over the top," Boggs said. "His longevity in the game speaks for itself. He's had no serious injuries and avoided banged up knees."

Yastrzemski and Boggs also took pride in their fielding ability. Yaz was a great left fielder. His catch to preserve, for the time being, Billy Rohr's no-hitter at Yankee Stadium in 1967 is a perfect example. It took time, but Boggs made himself into an excellent fielding third baseman.

Though he exhibited an ability to hit for power only one year in his career, that doesn't mean Boggs couldn't have done it on a regular basis. Eddie Popowski, a longtime member of the Boston organization, thought that if the Red Sox had asked Boggs to hit for more power he would have done so, and projected that the Sox might make that request because of the void left by Yaz' left-handed power bat. Yet either the Sox didn't press that issue, or Boggs followed to the beat of a different drummer, as he never became a consistent home run threat.

"He's the type of ballplayer that a club will look to for the big hit," Popowski said. As Boggs embarked on what was to be his Hall of Fame career, the veteran Sox coach hoped the Red Sox didn't try to adjust his hitting approach.. "He's a coachable kid," he said. " I hope they don't try to change him. That could screw up a hitter for the rest of his career. Though I think he's too smart to let that happen."

Manager Ralph Houk, who sat in his office chair reflecting on an unsuccessful season that was about to end, stated that Boggs was a different type of hitter than Yaz or Jim Rice. "He doesn't hit for power," Houk said, "He has proven he can hit all types of pitching. Boggs is a good Fenway Park hitter. For a young player, he's one of the most patient hitters I've ever seen. I've never seen a young player that's a better two-strike hitter."

Walt Hriniak, who served as pitching coach during some of Boggs' Boston tenure, was impressed immediately with the third baseman's hitting ability. "Boggs has tremendous discipline at the plate," he said. "He watches the ball longer than anybody in baseball. He came here a good hitter, and he's gotten better." He likened Boggs to Yastrzemski in that both have a "tremendous desire to be good."

During Boggs' rookie year in 1982, he didn't have enough plate appearances to qualify for the batting title, hitting .349 in 381 appearances, far short of the 502 appearances necessary to achieve that honor. "I thought if I could duplicate last year, I'd have a chance," he said. "When (Rod) Carew was hitting .400 at the All-Star break, I knew that he'd have to come down for me to win it." The Angels' Carew finished second at .339, well behind Boggs' .361.

Boggs and Hriniak worked well together because they were both disciples of the Charley Lau theory of hitting. "Basically, we have the same philosophy—to go through the middle, go the opposite way," Boggs said. The two men would spend at least a half hour before each game discussing who was pitching that day and what he threw. "I've always gone to the opposite field, even when I was in Little League," Boggs said.

As is the case with many great players, Boggs had his own personal idiosyncrasies. Boggs was considered one of the most superstitious players of his time. He ate chicken all the time, seven days a week. He didn't change the menu for his entire career, which led to the nickname "Chicken Man." He thought that it might affect his hitting if he started to add more variety to his menu.

Another sight fans noticed would be Boggs' appearance for batting practice at 5:17 p.m. and to run sprints on the field at 7:17 each night before a game, which started 13 minutes later. Not 7:16, not 7:18. Always the same time. He never deviated from it. Another example of being superstitious is that he always drew the Hebrew word "Chai," which means "life," in the batter's box in each at-bat, even though he wasn't Jewish.

Boggs actually asked legendary Fenway Park public address announcer Sherm Feller to refrain from announcing his number when he arrived at the plate for the rest of his Boston playing days. Boggs noticed that one time Feller had forgotten to say his number and that he broke out of a hitting slump shortly afterward. Again, superstition was something that was part of Boggs' personality.

It was ironic that when Wade Boggs reached the 3,000-hit plateau on August 7, 1999 the hit that made it possible was a home run. Boggs never sought home runs. He sought contact, hard contact, as he sprayed the ball around to all fields. The most home runs he ever hit in a season was 24 in 1987. It was by far the greatest total he had ever hit in a season. He never came close to that total again, averaging less than seven homers a season during his 18-year career.

Boggs was only the second player to have his 3,000[th] hit be a home run. In another touch of irony, Boggs hit the first home in the history of the Tampa franchise.

Of course, many Red Sox fans lament that Boggs didn't reach the 3,000-hit milestone in a Red Sox uniform. It seemed that Boggs might be a lifer on Lansdowne Street. Then came the scandal involving mistress Margo Adams in 1989 and an uncharacteristic .259 season in 1992, by far the worst campaign of his career. He departed the following year to New York to become a member of the hated Yankees. It became hard to watch for Sox fans as Boggs helped the Yankees win a World Series title in 1996, something Ted Williams never accomplished.

It should have happened for him earlier in '86 if it hadn't been for Bob Stanley, Bill Buckner, John McNamara, and some other usual suspects blamed from bar stools from Boston to Bangor. Many might recall that it was Boggs' double after Dave Henderson's go-ahead homer which enabled to Sox to take a two-run lead into the bottom of the 10th of what would have been a World Series-clinching victory over the Mets in Game 6 at Shea Stadium.

The world championship was in the bag, right? Sox owner Jean Yawkey knew better. She knew the long-suffering Red Sox history all too well. Asked to leave her seat prior to the bottom of the 10th inning to be part of the official presentation of the Series trophy in the Red Sox locker room, she declined. She had to actually see the last out. She wouldn't believe it until the last out was made, an out that never came.

For the first and only time in baseball history, a team came within one strike of losing the pennant and eventually won it (sorry, Gene Mauch), then came within one strike of winning the World Series and then lost (a plague on your house, Mr. McNamara).

An image of Boggs sobbing in the dugout after Game 7 at Shea Stadium is etched in our memories, another example of the Sox' star-crossed history. The Sox needed to win only one game of the last two at Yankee Stadium in 1949 to win the pennant. They couldn't do it. The previous year, the Sox lost a one-game playoff and the pennant to the Cleveland Indians.

The '86 Series debacle was just another example of bad Boston baseball luck. One Boston writer commented that "Red Sox fans know that the world will break their heart someday because each year they have it broken at Fenway Park."

One of the few bright spots of the disastrous 2015 Red Sox season was Brock Holt, a promising young player acquired from the Pirates in the 2012 winter deal that brought reliever Joel Hanrahan to Boston. Holt displayed excellent fielding and hitting skills during the club's disappointing last place follow-up to the surprising championship season of 2013. The Sox value him highly because he plays multiple positions, including third base.

He was named to the All-Star team in 2015. But some Sox fans had a problem with the number he was wearing. It was Boggs' 26. The Sox hadn't retired it yet, although Boggs was one of the greatest hitters in Red Sox history and was a skilled defensive third baseman. Inducted into the National Baseball Hall of Fame in 2005 with fellow infielder Ryne Sandberg of the Cubs, Boggs has a plaque that notes his .328 lifetime average, second on the Red Sox's all-time list behind Williams.

Manny Ramirez is probably the greatest right-handed hitter in Red Sox history. Williams holds that distinction from the left side of the plate. But Boggs and Carl Yastrzemski follow close behind. Boggs trails Williams by only six points in batting average as a Red Sox player, .338 to .344. And when the question is asked: What Red Sox player had the highest career average ever at Fenway Park? The answer is

Boggs at a staggering .369.

He led the Red Sox in hitting for *nine* consecutive seasons ('83-91), 10 if you add the partial year when he first came up to the Majors in '82.

After the Cardinals' Stan Musial retired in 1963 with a .331 career average, the players who retired with the next highest lifetime marks are Boggs and Carew, who also finished with a .328 career average.

The Sox never should have let Boggs go. Yes, there was a messiness and disappointment concerning the whole Margo affair, but was he the first ballplayer to fool around? Not by a long shot. And, yes, it was a bit more than just a brief fling.

The affair also resulted in Adams filing a lawsuit against Boggs, claiming he had reneged on a promise of money to offset the loss of income from her regular job when she travelled to cities where the Red Sox were playing..

He appeared on Barbara Walters' program to tell his side of the story, reportedly against the wishes of the Red Sox management. During the interview, Boggs told her he was a "sex addict." So he made a mistake and he dearly paid for it, but the guy didn't commit a felony, just poor judgment. His marriage didn't dissolve either. Let's put this in perspective.

The Red Sox did put him in the team's Hall of Fame in 2004 shortly before its national counterpart in Cooperstown gave Boggs his just recognition. There are now only 10 retired Red Sox numbers that are displayed on the façade of the right field deck at Fenway Park. They include Bobby Doerr (1), Joe Cronin (4) Johnny Pesky (6), Carl Yastrzemski (8) Ted Williams (9), Jim Rice (14), Carlton Fisk (27), Pedro Martinez (45), Boggs, and David Ortiz (34), whose number was retired in 2017.

All but Pesky and Ortiz are in Cooperstown. When "Big Papi" becomes eligible for enshrinement, it is likely he will get the necessary votes. For 11 seasons playing on the Olde Town Team, Boggs set a standard of play rarely seen. He was a hitting machine and made himself into a Gold Glove third baseman.

He left the game in 1999, having made 12-straight All-Star appearances at third base. Only Brooks Robinson and George Brett made more. On the day that Yastrzemski retired, Red Sox fans looked to Boggs to help step into the leadership role, along with Rice and a few others.

Although he certainly would have preferred reaching the 3,000-hit plateau in a Red Sox uniform, it must have been satisfying for Boggs to achieve that milestone in the place where it all began for him in Tampa, Florida, where his family moved when he was 11.

By 1976, his senior year at Plant High School, Boggs decided he wanted to concentrate on baseball and quit the football team, much to the dismay of the football coach. Even though Boggs had never kicked in a game before, he became the team's kicker, eventually making the all-state team in that capacity.

While Red Sox fans can debate who the better pure hitter was, Williams or Boggs, it should be understood that there would have likely been no Boggs had there not been a Williams. Wade's father Win, who was a major influence in his son's life and development as a player, bought Williams' book *The Science of Hitting* and highlighted several passages for Wade to read. Suddenly, Boggs' hitting fortunes improved dramatically, even though Williams was a pull hitter and Boggs favored going the other way when the ball was pitched away from him. Williams' overriding belief concerning hitting was a simple approach: Get a good pitch to hit.

When he was elected to the Baseball Hall of Fame, Boggs could only marvel at how far the kid from Tampa had come. "There is not a word to describe what it means," he said. "Unbelievable doesn't work. I wish they would invent a new word."

Little did he know that when the Red Sox finally retired his number, appropriately on the 26th of May, Sandberg would emerge from the Red Sox dugout to be a part of the ceremony. The two Hall of Famers, who had shared their special day in Cooperstown, embraced. He was clearly touched that Sandberg made the effort to be there at Fenway.

The Red Sox know how to do this type of thing. Even the placement of the microphone for the speakers at the ceremony was at the right spot, third base—real estate Boggs had patrolled his entire career in Boston.

A smart move on the team's part was to honor the ill-fated '86 Red Sox the night before. Thus several members of that team stayed around another night for the Boggs ceremony, including Worcester's Rich Gedman, and Marty Barrett, Dwight Evans, Dennis "Oil Can" Boyd, and fellow Hall of Famers Rice and Yastrzemski, who had perhaps the greatest all-around season of any Red Sox player when he won the Triple Crown and played Gold Glove left field for the '67 pennant-winning Sox.

Yaz, who rarely appears at Fenway these days, knew how good Boggs was and admired his work ethic, something that was part of his own DNA. Yaz got every bit out of his ability and knew that Boggs did too. Neither was an imposing physical specimen.

Boggs was clearly emotional appearing at Fenway after his number joined other Sox immortals. "I think I said it best out there that this was the last piece of my baseball puzzle," he told the crowd in a pre-game ceremony. "My journey has ended and I've come back home. This is where I started my career, and today is the end. To have my number up there with all the greats to ever put on a Red Sox uniform, including Ted (Williams), my idol growing up. I wore number 9 in honor of Ted in Little League."

On another occasion Boggs recalled meeting the "Splendid Splinter" shortly after he had been drafted by the Red Sox. He was close to him in a movie line in Florida, where Ted had a home. He introduced himself. Once Williams heard Boggs was a Red Sox draft pick, they immediately began to talk about hitting. This was heaven for Boggs. Later, after Boggs became a star, he and Yankees' first baseman Don Mattingly received an invitation from Ted to join him one evening after a spring training game. Again, Boggs was in heaven. The reverence for Williams remains to this day.

Williams' death greatly saddened him. Both of his parents are gone now. He recalled losing his mother Sue during his Red Sox career, getting the word when the Red Sox were playing a series at Yankee Stadium that she died in an automobile accident. During the number retirement ceremony, he looked at former hitting coach Walt Hriniak and thanked him for helping him get through that difficult time.

"My father was instrumental," he said at the ceremony. "He was my hitting coach. He was alive in 2005 when I went to the Hall of Fame. My mother was killed in '86. They were smiling down on me today. They were sitting at the table with Ted smiling down. They had the front row seats and they got to see it. When the Red Sox covering came off of the number and I pointed up and I blew my Mom a kiss, I didn't think I could hold it together then. But somehow I did. Very emotional."

Boggs said that he didn't think his induction into the Baseball Hall of Fame could be topped, but he told the Sox fans that the number retirement had done just that. "For a player to have their number retired is not a right, it's a privilege; it's the highest honor any player can receive from an organization. In closing, my number may live up there forever with all the greats to put on a Red Sox uniform, but you, the great fans of Boston, will be forever in my heart. Thank you for sharing this wonderful day with me and my family."

CHAPTER 7

ROGER CLEMENS

Roger Clemens was interviewed in the Red Sox locker room prior to a game in late September of 1986. He was completing a breakthrough season for him, which also was one of the greatest pitching performances in Red Sox history.

At that time he had won 23 games. He would add one more victory to that total before the regular season's end, capture his first Cy Young Award and also be named MVP. Later that season, during the American League Championship Series and World Series, triumph and tragedy—the latter being the team's hallmark in a 68-year World Series title drought—would again be on display.

Little did he know that six more Cy Young awards would follow or that his legacy would later be tainted by accusations of steroid use that would bar his entry, perhaps forever, into Baseball's Hall of Fame. The opening part of this chapter captures the story resulting from my clubhouse meeting with him as it was published on September 20, 1986. Following that are some further comments about the Red Sox and Clemens' long and controversial career.

7

A Rocket Blasts Off But Has A Bumpy Re-entry

WHEN BOSTON RED Sox fans recall the glorious season of 1986, many individual performances will stand out. But one effort will clearly rise above them all—Roger Clemens' mastery on the pitching mound.

Clemens has not only been the story of the Red Sox this season, he has been the story in baseball. He has been, quite simply, the most dominant pitcher in both leagues, starting out the season with an unbeaten streak of 14 games, including a record-setting 20-strikeout game against the Seattle Mariners in April.

The 24-year-old hurler from Katy, Texas is the stopper Boston has needed for many years and the anchor of a pitching staff boasting the second-best American League earned run average (3.89 as of last Sunday). He has stopped losing streaks in 13 of 15 possible opportunities. A Clemens victory is almost automatic, reminding one of Ron Guidry's 25-3 performance in'78.

Clemens' latest effort as a stopper came Tuesday night when the Sox beat the Milwaukee Brewers, 2-1, in the first game of a doubleheader. He struck out 10 batters, the eighth time he had struck out 10 or more this season, tying Jim Lonborg for the club single season record. The victory raised his record to 23-4 and lowered his earned run average to 2.56.

When the University of Texas product arrived at Red Sox spring training in Winter Haven, Florida in 1984, club officials knew they had something special. Then manager Ralph Houk, went so far as to call him the "best pitching prospect I've ever seen." There was no doubt that he would win 20 games someday; the question was when?

But many didn't envision that Clemens would be *this* good. He has a chance to hold Red Sox modern-day single season pitching records for wins, winning percentage, and strikeouts. A 26-victory season would vault him past Dave "Boo" Ferris, who was 25-6 in 1946. Ferris also holds the best winning percentage with .806 for that season. Clemens has 227 strikeouts and is within reach of Lonborg's mark of 246 set in 1967.

Smoky Joe Wood holds the all-time Red Sox pitching records in those categories, setting all of them in 1912, the year Fenway Park opened. Wood had 34 wins, a .872 winning percentage, and 258 strikeouts.

Asked if he ever expected the type of year he's had, Clemens said, "You don't expect some of the wonderful things that are happening. I don't know about anybody else, but I expect to do well. When I got out there I'm trying to do great things. I've put in a lot of hard work to get to this position and I'm just trying to keep going. There's no time to let up now."

Red Sox fans were concerned whether Clemens could stay healthy this season after undergoing surgery on his right shoulder last August. Clemens didn't share their concern.

"I didn't have any doubts about coming back," he said. "I was told by a lot of qualified physicians that my surgery was very minor and they said it would be nothing but a 100 percent outcome, and that seems to be the case."

Clemens had some cartilage removed from his shoulder, a condition that some speculated was caused by pitching too many innings. The affable 6-4, 215-pound pitcher agreed that he'd pitched a great number of innings, but didn't believe that was the reason for the injury.

"When I got to the minor leagues I started throwing the ball consistently harder," he said. "I'd been pitching 12 years. One of the doctors said it even might have been caused by a hit in football, the way the cartilage was torn. It tore a little farther and started rubbing in the joint and that's what caused the discomfort."

He has become smarter about the care of his arm. He was introduced to wrist weights by Red Sox team physician Arthur Pappas and lifts them daily to strengthen the rotator cuff. The rotator cuff consists of four main muscles in the arm.

"Dr. Pappas says if I keep doing it religiously I'm going to keep on getting stronger and stronger," Clemens said. "I'm throwing the ball as hard as I've ever thrown it. I threw it 100 mph in Detroit and 99 in the All-Star Game. So right now it seems to be getting better."

That's a scary proposition for American League batters, who have been swinging and missing at Clemens' fastball all season. Fenway Park bleacher fans have brought signs with the letter "K" on them, placing a sign on the wall with each strikeout victim. The crowd is noticeably aroused when he gets two strikes on a batter.

Red Sox pitching coach Bill Fischer, greatly respected for his handling of pitchers, said Clemens' performance this year is the best he's ever seen. "You knew he had ability, but how many guys are 23-4?" he said.

Fischer never witnessed a winning streak like Clemens' (April 11 to June 27) and was equally impressed with the way he pitched after the streak was broken.

"A lot of guys would go through a streak like that and fall flat on their face in the second half," he said. "He hasn't done that."

Some other pitchers can throw hard, but Clemens has proven that he is pitcher, not just a thrower. "He's got a curve and a slider," Fischer said. "He can pitch. He moves the ball around." The coach said Clemens will win the Cy Young Award "as sure as the sun comes up in the morning."

Pitching is the difference in the Red Sox this season. For the first time in many years, fans are coming to see pitching as much as hitting at Fenway.

"For all the years around here they'd pound the ball and they wouldn't win," Fischer said. "Why?" Fischer said, leaving the obvious answer—inadequate pitching—unspoken.

For all his achievements and personal glories, Clemens never puts himself above the interest of the team's success, a quality that always goes over well in the locker room.

"You have to have a team unified or you're not going to any-where," Clemens said. "If everybody isn't pulling for everybody else at all times there's going to be a wheel missing. You need four wheels to make the car to go. It's always been team first and me second and if you keep it that way you're going to win a lot of ballgames."

He will say that he needed the team's help to gain all 23 of his victories, but sometimes it seemed like he could have gone out there alone and won.

He's been rolling sevens all season and there's no reason to be-lieve his good fortune is going to stop soon.

––––––––

So that was Roger Clemens in the fall of 1986 just prior to his first post-season experience. That experience began badly, as he was on the mound when the Sox lost the opening game of the American League Championship Series in a lopsided California Angels 8-1 vic-tory, with starter Mike Witt gaining the win. He pitched shutout ball into the ninth inning of Game 4 in Anaheim, but a fielding miscue by Jim Rice and reliever Calvin Schiraldi's first poor playoff performance put the Angels within one win of the pennant. Then came the famous Dave Henderson home run in the ninth inning of Game 5, which saved Boston's season, leading to two blowout wins in Boston.

Angels reliever Donnie Moore, who gave up the Henderson home run, was devastated and committed suicide three years later. Moore needed just one more strike to seal the Angels' win. The Red Sox soon would come to know the same type of painful experience in the World Series.

Clemens pitched impressively in an 8-1 Sox victory in Game 7 to pave the Red Sox' way to the World Series. And although the Rocket pitched well in the World Series overall, he didn't record a victory, as he was strangely lifted before the fifth inning of Game 2, a 9-3 Red Sox win. Questions abounded again when Clemens was replaced for a pinch hitter after seven innings in the memorable Game 6. Manager John McNamara said that he asked to be taken out of the game, which Clemens disputes.

Anyway, we all know how that worked out: Despite Henderson hitting another meaningful home run and Boston adding one more tally in the 10th, the Mets rallied for three runs with two outs in the bottom of the inning, eventually winning the game on the infamous Bill Buckner error.

Despite pitching for the Sox for another decade, Clemens never made it to another World Series in a Boston uniform. He did win two more Cy Young awards while pitching for the Sox, posting records of 20-9 in 1987 and 18-10 in 1991. He finished third in Cy Young voting in 1992 with a similar 18-11 record. In the four years that followed he never won more than 11 games and his earned run average was over 4.0 in two of those four years. General Manager Dan Duquette felt that Clemens' best years were behind him and the numbers didn't seem to dispute that. He memorably said that at 34 Clemens was in "the twilight of his career." Clemens' weight had ballooned from 200 to 240 pounds in those last Sox years, which didn't help his pitching.

No one should fault the Red Sox for not matching what the Toronto Blue Jays gave the Texan, a three-year, $24.5 million contract, with incentives that provided an opportunity to boost that total to $31.1 million. Boston was not going to pay that type of money at that stage of Clemens' career. And who can blame Clemens for heading North? The package was the richest ever given a pitcher and it appeared that the Blue Jays had overpaid for Clemens. Boston had made a late bid of $22 million over four years, which lagged behind some suitors other than the Blue Jays for Clemens' services.

Yet, the Boston media had a field day when the signing was announced. Scribes had a good point when they criticized Red Sox management for allowing Clemens to become a free agent and not signing him in his walk year for considerably less money.

But the sharpest barbs were aimed at Clemens himself. *Boston Globe* columnist Mike Barnicle called Clemens "a complete dope" and added that "you would not for a single second—even with his guaranteed contract—want your child to grow up to like Roger Clemens: selfish, spoiled, and seriously deficient in character."

The words "arrogance, "greed," and "betrayal" were applied to Clemens by many Boston fans at the time. Clemens had talked about wanting to stay with the Red Sox, indicating that the only other place he would consider playing was back home in Texas. There was some consolation that Clemens didn't sign with the hated Yankees. But then Sox fans faced what they considered the ultimate indignity two years later when he donned pinstripes, employing an opt-out clause included in the Toronto contract.

Another *Globe* columnist, Dan Shaughnessey, wrote, "Clemens today is a villain in Boston and it didn't have to be that way. He worked hard and did a good job for most of his career. But his departure lacked grace and dignity. No doubt Sox fans will return the compliment when he comes through town next July." But Shaughnessey also said he would miss Clemens, who had been a fixture on the team so many years, and his colorful personality and pitching prowess.

A headline on top of George Kimball's column in *The Boston Herald* screamed "Clemens Not Worth It." The Herald also heaped blame on the Red Sox front office for allowing Clemens to get away. Clemens' agents, the Hendricks brothers, told the *Herald* they knew the Sox didn't want Clemens to return based on their initial low offer, which was reportedly two years guaranteed at $10 million each, plus another two years and $10 million through incentives.

It was difficult at the time for any knowledgeable baseball fan to believe he would win any more Cy Young Awards, let alone four. He showed up on the mound in Toronto in April with a different-looking body. He had dropped the excess weight and appeared more muscular and in terrific shape. Clemens won the Cy Young Award in both of his two seasons in Toronto before exercising the contract option to join the Yankees.

Jose Canseco, a former Boston teammate, was a member of the Blue Jays when he arrived. Canseco later stated in a book that both he and Clemens used steroids in Toronto. Clemens denied that he used any performance-enhancing drugs. But based on his final years in Boston, compared to what he went on to accomplish after he left the Hub, many were skeptical.

The Mitchell Report, headed by former Maine Senator George Mitchell, named Clemens numerous times as a suspected steroid user, citing testimony given by Clemens' former trainer Brian McNamee.

Former Yankee and Houston Astro teammate Andy Pettitte testified in a trial in 2012 that Clemens had told him that he used human growth hormone in 1999. Clemens said that Pettitte had "misremembered" the conversation and again denied taking such a substance. How do you "misremember" a revelation like that? The trial, in which Clemens was being prosecuted for lying to Congress, amazingly resulted in his acquittal on all six counts.

Clemens and other stars such as Mark McGuire and Barry Bonds are considered by many fans to be poster boys of the Steroid Era in baseball. One of the side effects of steroid use can be an enlarged head. That wasn't the case with Clemens, but Bonds looked like a human bobblehead doll in the final years of his career.

There is much debate about whether Clemens and other notable players of the Steroid Era deserve to be in the Hall of Fame. After Bud Selig—Commissioner during that era—was selected for Hall induction in 2017, some writers believe they would have justification voting for Clemens and Bonds.

Houston's Jeff Bagwell and Texas catcher Ivan Rodriguez had been rumored to have taken steroids and yet gained Hall election in 2017, but Clemens and Bonds fell far short. The controversy surrounding the latter two was much greater than that involving Bagwell and Rodriguez. Bonds was even convicted of obstruction of justice related to an investigation of performance-enhancing drugs, though not of actually taking them. He served 30 days in jail.

One Boston writer predicted that the fact that Clemens and Bonds had crossed the 50 percent threshold for the first time in 2017 was an indication that they definitely would be inducted sometime in their remaining years of eligibility. Clemens was named on 54.1 percent of the ballots, Bonds, 53.8 percent. Being named on at least 75 percent of the ballots is needed and both Bonds and Clemens have been reaping a higher amount of vote with each year of eligibility.

But the latest 2018 Hall of Fame voting results showed that Clemens and Bonds had made little progress, with Clemens gaining 57.3 percent of the vote and Bonds 56.4. They have four more years of eligibility.

When "Shoeless" Joe Jackson was banned from baseball after the

1919 "Black Sox Scandal," he had never been found guilty of foul play in a court of law, nor were the teammates who actually helped "fix" the Series. Jackson knew about the plan and remained silent, while having an outstanding Series statistically. Yet one doesn't necessarily have to be found guilty in a court of law to be deemed guilty by many people in the court of public opinion. Just ask O.J. Simpson.

All of the "Black Sox" involved in gambler Arnold Rothstein's fix were banned from baseball, their reputations tarnished forever. After a controversial acquittal in the criminal case involving the murder of his wife and her friend, Simpson was found guilty of the same crime in a civil suit. Paroled from prison in 2017 after serving nine years for an unrelated crime, Simpson remains a polarizing figure.

What would the message be to youngsters if Clemens and Bonds were able to gain entry? Cheat if you can find a way to get away with breaking the rules—you might end up in the Hall of Fame. *Saturday Night Live* once satirized the use of performance-enhancing drugs in the Olympics. The sketch showed a weightlifter about to perform, with the announcer stating that the competition was taking place at the "All-Drug Olympics" in which athletes could take anything they wanted if they felt it would give them an edge. Where would sports in America be if *that* permissive attitude toward drugs was common?

The sad thing is that Clemens, with his three Cy Young Awards already on his mantelpiece and two 20-strikeout games, had a good case for Hall induction based on his years in a Red Sox uniform. He may have to settle for being a member of the Boston team's Hall of Fame. The Red Sox inducted him in 2014, but haven't retired his number. That honor is usually reserved for those who are found in Cooperstown. David Ortiz received that honor the year after he retired before being eligible for the Hall, so the Sox could have retired Clemens' 21 by now, but declined.

The Clemens testimony before Congress was satirized in a fictional anonymous work printed below that circulated around the Internet. It provided a humorous "alternate testimony" that reminded one of a famous Jack Nicholson movie scene:

CLEMENS: I have prepared a statement that I would like to read into the record. I've been asked to appear before this committee because you in Congress have been saying you are seeking the truth about the use of steroids and human growth hormone in baseball. It is my belief that you can't HANDLE the truth.

Ladies and gentleman we live in a world that has baseballs. And those balls have to be hit by men with bats. Who's going to do it? YOU, Congressman? I have a greater responsibility than you can possibly fathom. You weep for steroids and you curse HGH. You have that luxury. You have the luxury of not knowing what I know: that HGH, while illegal, probably sells tickets. And my existence, while grotesque and incomprehensible to you, sells tickets.

You don't want the truth, because deep down, in places you don't talk about at parties, you want me on that mound. You need me on that mound. We use words like fastball, slider, splitfinger...We use these words as the backbone of a life spent playing a sport. You use them as a punchline.

I have neither the time nor the inclination to explain myself to a man who rises and falls asleep to Sports Center video clips I provide, then questions the manner in which I provide them. I'd rather you just say, "Thank you" and went on your way. Otherwise, I suggest you pick up a bat and dig in. Either way, I don't give a damn what you think you're entitled to.

CHAPTER 8

JOHNNY SAIN

Johnny Sain came out of a small Arkansas town in the Ozark Mountains and became an outstanding pitcher and pitching coach. He pitched for the Boston Braves, New York Yankees, and Kansas City Athletics from 1942-55, with a three-year break while in the service during World War II, and later acted as a pitching coach for the Yankees, Twins, Tigers, and White Sox.

When Sain's playing career came to a close, the Baseball Hall of Fame wasn't something he thought much about. He once joked, "You don't put a mule in a stable of thoroughbreds." But as time passed, Sain looked at the entirety of his career and began to feel that induction wasn't such a far-fetched idea after all.

It was after he retired from baseball that we met the day before the opening of an autograph show in Sturbridge, Massachusetts in July of 1990. He was an affable man whose physical stature a writer once likened to a "cigar store Indian, tall and erect."

I found that Sain carried around copies of newspaper clippings, magazine articles, and other information, all of which he shared with me, greatly contributing to the shape of this chapter. He told me that treasure trove of information would help me tell his story.

When he died at 89 in 2006, his dream of Hall induction had not been realized, and that remains, sadly, unchanged.

8

Pray For Rain And
The Hall of Fame

THE FIELD IS still there, but it's now home to Boston University athletics. What was once the right field grandstand, as well as a nearby plaque, are the only reminders of its former tenant and the site's place in Boston sports history.

One wonders if the ghosts of baseball seasons past still hover over this place once known as Braves Field and where a special magic existed during the summer of 1948 when the Boston Braves won their second and final National League pennant.

For Boston baseball fans, the summer of '48 will be remembered as much as the following summer chronicled by the late author David Halberstam in *Summer of '49*, when the other team in town, the more popular Red Sox, lost the pennant to the Yankees on the last day of the season. The Sox had lost a one-game playoff to Lou Boudreau's Cleveland Indians at Fenway Park in '48, the only time Hub fans came that close to a subway Series.

When people remember the '48 Braves, two people come to mind instantly: Warren Spahn and Johnny Sain. During the pennant drive that September, it seemed to Braves' fans that the two men hurled every other game. Not exactly, but during a 12-game period beginning on Labor Day, in which Spahn and Sain posted victories in a doubleheader sweep, the two pitchers combined for an 8-0 record.

That amazing accomplishment was aided by the schedule, some rained out games, and the hurlers being used at times on short rest.

The popular chant became "Spahn and Sain, then pray for rain." The rallying cry came from the title of a poem written by *Boston Post* sports editor Gerald Hern, which was published on September 14th of that year. The poem read:

First, we'll use Spahn
then we'll use Sain
Then an off day
followed by rain
Back will come Spahn
followed by Sain
And followed
we hope
by two days of rain

Spahn is in the Hall of Fame after posting an incredible 363 victories over a 21-year career, while Sain, who collected considerably less career wins (139) in 11 seasons is not enshrined in Cooperstown. But when one looks at the entire picture of Sain's career as both a player and coach, it's hard to understand why his plaque isn't in Cooperstown as well.

During the summer of '48, Sain was one of the National League's best pitchers. He had 24 wins (24-15), made 39 starts and completed 28 games—leading the league in all three categories. His earned run average was 2.60, ranking third in the league. He was the runner-up to the Cardinals' great Stan Musial in the Most Valuable Player Voting.

This was the year of Sain, not Spahn. Spahn pitched well, but his 15-12 record and 3.71 ERA—along with 16 complete games—didn't compare with Sain's numbers. Spahn's ERA that season was his highest in the 18-year stretch from '46 to '63. Spahn had led the league in '47 with a 2.33 mark.

During the pennant drive, the small-town boy from Havana, Arkansas pitched eight complete games in 10 starts during the season's last 29 games—quite a feat. Can you imagine anyone doing that today?

Said said his greatest thrill in baseball was besting Cleveland's

Bob Feller, 1-0, in Game 1 of the '48 Series at Braves Field. In Game 4 of the Series, he pitched well again, but the Braves lost, 2-1. He would have pitched the seventh game, but the Indians won the title in six games.

Watching Sain in those two starts, Hall of Famer Tris Speaker writing for a newspaper, praised the Boston right-hander. Speaker compared Sain to another Hall of Famer, Christy Mathewson. "Johnny Sain is a great pitcher," Speaker wrote, "one of the finest I ever saw in World Series competition...I don't say that Sain is a great pitcher because he throws a blazing fastball or a startling curve or is a 'freak pitcher.' I say he's great because he knows how to adapt his pitching to a situation."

After Sain's performance against Feller in the Series, Braves manager Bill Southworth heaped praised on his pitcher. "He was pitching under pressure from start to finish, especially at the finish," Southworth said. "But John Sain, as all of the 40,000 crowd knows, is at this best when facing his hardest assignments. Sain, I realize, knew what he was in for when facing Bob Feller. So he went all out as he had previously this season on so many occasions."

The great Cy Young saw the '48 Series and also came away impressed. "Sain has the right idea," said the then 81-year-old Young. "You can't do it all by pitching straight overhand. When I came up in the '90s, I had thought I had a good overhand fastball and a good overhand curve. But that wasn't enough to get batters like (Cap) Anson, (Sam) Crawford, and (Ed) Delahanty out, or the young fellow that came up with the Tigers, Ty Cobb. So I started throwing sidearm—the way Sain did today—and found that was just what I needed. I kept 'em low, and that's Sain all over."

Comparing to the present era of six and seven-inning starting pitchers, Sain completed 57 percent of his career starts and an amazing 71 percent in '48. In contrast, the Red Sox' Roger Clemens completed only five games during his 24-4 gem of a season in '86. The Boston Braves' hurler led the league in complete games again with 24 and 28, respectively, in '46 and '48.

Of course, the game has changed, with relief pitchers playing a more prominent role now, and most starters throwing harder than they did in Sain's day. Pitching on three days rest, let alone two, has become virtually extinct. It's clear that pitchers were asked to do more during the '40s and '50s, both in finishing the game and pitching on fewer days rest.

Clemens, whose suspected performance-enhancing drug use has delayed, perhaps forever, his Hall of Fame entry—posted five 20-game seasons. Along with his '48 performance, Sain compiled records of 20-14 in '46, 21-12 in '47, and 20-13 in '50.

Another thing Sain was required to do that American league pitchers don't do anymore is hit, unless they are playing an inter-league game at a National League ballpark. Sain was an accomplished hitter. He was the only player during the '40s to win 20 games and bat over .300 during the same season.

His finest year at the plate was in '47, when he hit .356 in 107 at-bats. Sain led the league in sacrifice bunts in '48. He finished with a career batting average of .245 and struck out only 11 times in 11 seasons, an amazing statistic. That's approximately every 30 at-bats. Managers considered Sain a viable option as a pinch hitter.

Sain was traded to the Yankees in '51 and was a member of three World Series championship teams. Used primarily as a relief pitcher, he led the league in saves in '54 with 26.

Like many players of his era, he lost some prime baseball years due to military service. As a rookie for the Braves, he compiled a 4-7 record, returning from war in '46 to win 65 games in three years. His career record was 139-116, an even 100 coming with the Braves. We'll never know whether he would have won at least 61 games during those war years, bringing him to the 200-win mark. His career ERA is 3.49.

Then again, one wonders whether he would have become the same pitcher had he not entered the service. He trained as an Air Cadet at Amherst College with crosstown rivals Ted Williams and Johnny Pesky in '42.

Sain told Braves' owner Lou Perini that he didn't waste any of his free time while serving his country. "When other flyers used their free time to go into town or play cards or just loaf, I was throwing a baseball," he said. "If I could get somebody to catch I threw to a human receiver. If I couldn't find anyone I was throwing at a target on the back of buildings. Mr. Perini, I believe I left dents in buildings in every station I was sent. I worked hard, and I found that I had something."

The Hall of Fame Veterans Committee, the only group that can enshrine Sain with baseball's immortals, should not penalize him for having served his country honorably. This is a problem for some other players as well who should be seriously considered, but aren't because they were unable to build up their statistics during the war years. It's a major flaw in the selection process that should be remedied. To go by total wins in Sain's case is ludicrous.

The Hall induction of Dennis Eckersley might be regarded as a somewhat comparable situation. Eckersley's 24 playing years were more than twice the number of Sain's. But combining his starting and relief roles, Eckersley ended with a record of 197-171 and a 3.50 ERA. True, Eckersley was a dominant reliever for more years than Sain, but he also didn't have the same success as a starter nor the coaching credentials that Sain does, or hitting prowess.

The question should be: Was he one of the best pitchers of the '40s?

And if there is some doubt in the minds of committee members about whether Sain belongs for his performance as a player, the man's status as perhaps the greatest pitching coach all time should punch his ticket to Cooperstown.

During his 14-year tenure as pitching coach for the Yankees, Twins, Tigers, and White Sox, he guided pitchers to 16 seasons of 20 victories or more.

Baseball had not seen a 30-game winner in 34 years prior to the '68 season, which was the "Year of the Pitcher," as Detroit's Denny McClain won 31 games. Sain was his pitching coach. There hasn't been a 30-game winner since. McLain won 24 games the next year under Sain's direction. Those two seasons were without question McClain's best.

"Sain taught me that the only way to accomplish great ideas is thinking about them persistently and to never stop learning," McLain told a reporter. "When I saw a 50-year-old man like him still carrying around schoolbooks, I knew I could still learn something."

Hall of Famer Whitey Ford won 12 games for the Yankees in 1960 and never won 20 until Sain arrived as Yankees' pitching coach the following year. He won 25 games in '61 and 24 more in '63.

Ford told the press, "Early in my career I was a fastball, curve, and change-up pitcher. In '61 when Johnny came over as pitching coach, he suggested that I experiment with a sinker and slider. I was able to baffle batters with those pitches. I think I won 67 games in the three years he was pitching coach." (He was close. It was 66.)

Numerous pitchers won 20 games for the first time under Sain, and never won 20 after he left as pitching coach, Ford being one of them. Others who first reached that milestone under Sain's tutelage include Ralph Terry, Jim Bouton, Jim "Mudcat" Grant, Jim Kaat, Earl Wilson, McLain, Wilbur Wood, and Stan Bahnsen.

Kaat might be the best example of Sain's influence. He won 25 games under Sain in '66 with the Twins and 21 and 20 under Sain's guidance in '74 and '75, respectively, for the White Sox. Kaat pitched 25 seasons, and those were the ones he reached the 20-win plateau.

Bouton had great admiration for Sain, calling him the "the most outstanding person I ever met." The former Yankee, whose nickname was "Bulldog," faded into oblivion after Sain's departure and is best remembered for his eye-opening book *Ball Four*, which exposed the private lives of players during the season. When Sain was dismissed as Yankees pitching coach over what was reportedly a $2,500 salary dispute, Bouton commented that he would have paid Sain out of his own pocket.

Wood's transformation was stark. He posted a 4.54 ERA in '69. A year later, under Sain's guidance, he lowered it to 3.12, and he thrived pitching on two days rest (a Sain recommendation), winning 22 games in '70. He won 24 in both '72 and '73 and 20 in '74.

Sain departed from the conventional practice of encouraging pitchers to run between starts, believing that most pitchers needed the three-day recovery time after a start. Instead, he recommended spending that time working on another pitch that could be added to their repertoire. Fooling the hitter was an important part of pitching, Sain believed, and that adding another pitch could make a big difference. Changing speeds and deliveries was something Sain did as a pitcher, and he preached the same gospel to his disciples.

Former Atlanta Braves pitching coach Leo Mazzone guided Hall of Famers Tom Glavine, John Smoltz, and Greg Maddux. Sain entrusted all his notes and pitching theories to Mazzone, who told *The Sporting News*, "Johnny was a bit of a rebel. He believed in throwing a lot and running a little. He believed in hanging with his pitchers only. He believed in making them first-class citizens."

Dick Radatz, the former great Red Sox reliever whose nickname was "The Monster," had lost his confidence before Sain took him under his wing as the Tigers' pitching coach. That changed and Radatz became a more effective reliever again in '69.

Sain believed it is unfair that several managers are in the Hall of Fame, but no coaches are. For instance, Charlie Lau and Walt Hriniak, recognized as among the greatest hitting coaches of all time, aren't enshrined in Cooperstown.

There are two other historical facts about Sain that put him in a unique place in baseball history. He was the last player to pitch to Babe Ruth in a game (an exhibition contest) and the first to pitch to Jackie Robinson as he broke the color line with the Brooklyn Dodgers in April of '47.

Sain's name was written on only 2.4 percent of the Hall ballots in 1969, representing eight votes, during his last year of eligibility—far short of the 75 percent required. Musial and Robinson's teammate, Roy Campanella, were inducted that year. The Veterans Committee voted to induct two pitchers, the Cleveland Indians' Stan Coveleski and the Yankees' Waite Hoyt.

Let's hope the Veterans Committee takes another look at Sain's entire body of work, which would mean allowing an exception to the usual criteria when it is merited. Sain's career, after all, was exceptional in so many ways.

CHAPTER 9

JACK CHESBRO

One day I was browsing through a copy of *Sports Illustrated* and found a section about the most successful athletes produced by each state. On the Massachusetts list, I found Jack Chesbro of North Adams. The fact that he was a North Adams native immediately caught my eye because I had spent my college years there at North Adams State College, now known as the Massachusetts College of Liberal Arts.

But who was Jack Chesbro?

I decided to find out more about him, pouring through articles and newspaper clippings. I encountered an interesting character, who was elected to the Baseball Hall of Hall in 1946, a decision that is debated even today. This chapter focuses on these two points of view and also provides more detail about Chesbro's life and playing career.

9

In Search Of "Happy Jack"

BILL JAMES IS widely regarded as a master analyst of baseball's past, but it's not difficult to disagree when he downplays the accomplishments of John Dwight Chesbro, better known as Jack Chesbro or his nickname "Happy Jack."

Most baseball fans never heard of him, yet he's in the National Baseball Hall of Fame. Part of the reason is that Chesbro pitched at the beginning of the 20th century at the start of what is defined as the "modern era" of professional baseball. A native of North Adams, Massachusetts, he is one of only two players born in Berkshire County to be inducted, the other being Negro League star second baseman Frank Grant of Pittsfield, who played in white professional baseball briefly before the color line was drawn in 1887.

Chesbro is one of only 10 players in the Hall born in Massachusetts and one of only four pitching inductees who are natives of the Bay State. Two of those pitchers, John Clarkson and Tim Keefe, played in the 1880s and '90s. Former Atlanta Braves star Tom Glavine, born in Concord and later a resident of Billerica, is the only other Massachusetts inductee who pitched after 1900.

Chesbro's biggest claim to fame is that he holds the modern record for wins in his magical season of 1904. Playing for the New York Highlanders, a team which was renamed the Yankees in 1913, Chesbro won 41 games. He also led the American League in winning percentage (.774), games pitched (55) and started (51), complete games (48), and innings (454 2/3). He was second in strikeouts (239) and fifth in earned run average (1.82). He still holds the franchise season record for wins, games started, complete games, and innings.

That year marked the fourth time he had won at least 20 games. He reached that mark two years later for the fifth and final time in 1906, posting a 24-16 record. In 1901 and 1902, he had records of 21-9 and 28-6 for the National League's Pittsburgh Pirates and was 21-15 in 1903 for the Highlanders.

Yet James is not impressed, noting that Chesbro had five other mediocre to poor seasons. He writes that Chesbro's greatest seasons were not really so great because winning 20 games didn't mean as much as it does today, arguing that winning 30 games was more the standard for excellence than 20.

That argument loses credibility when one compares Chesbro's record against his peers during his best seasons. Consider the fact that the pitcher in the American League with the second most wins in 1904 was Boston's Cy Young with 27. Chesbro had *14* more wins than the next pitcher on the list. That's amazing. It's similar to Babe Ruth leading the American League in home runs in 1919 with 29, while three hitters followed him on the list, each with 10.

James *is* correct in noting that more pitchers reached the 20-win plateau in Chesbro's day. The fact that the four-man rotation was used during that time, giving pitchers more starts, influenced this. But winning 20 games still set a pitcher apart from most of his contemporaries.

Young, who recorded an astounding 511 victories in his career, never came close to posting 41 wins in a season, his best attempt being a 35-victory season for the National League's Cleveland Spiders in 1895. In an effort to find a player comparable to Chesbro, James selected former New York Mets pitcher Jerry Koosman in his *Baseball Historical Abstract*.

Jerry Koosman had some fine seasons, being most remembered as a member of the 1969 "Miracle" Mets, but the comparison is lacking on several fronts.

While Chesbro holds the distinction of having led both the National and American leagues in 1902 and 1904 in wins, respectively, Koosman never reached that pinnacle in either league. He did have the dubious distinction of leading both leagues in losses, 20 with the Mets in '77 and 13 with the Minnesota Twins in '81.

Reviewing his five best seasons, Koosman is entirely missing from the league's pitching category leaders during one of those seasons, '74. In his other notable seasons, 1968, '69, '76, and '79, the best he could do was tie for second in the National League in wins (21). In '68 he was not among the top six in winning percentage, while not placing in the top four in wins in '69.

Chesbro's and Koosman's career win total *are* similar. Koosman actually has 23 more victories at 222-209 than Chesbro did with a 199-127 record. But Koosman played 19 seasons, compared with Chesbro's 11, and started almost 200 more games than Chesbro. His career winning percentage of .515 is almost 100 points less than Chesbro's .610. Koosman reached the 20-win plateau twice.

Was winning 30 games more indicative of excellence? During Chesbro's five best seasons, two in the National League and three in the American League, only three pitchers other than Chesbro—Young, and the New York Giants' Joe McGinnity and Christy Mathewson—reached the 30-win mark. Young and McGinnity did it twice and Mathewson once. All three are in the Hall of Fame.

James is right in making the statement that Chesbro holds the modern record for Major League wins in a season because "someone drew a line" behind him at the turn of the century to begin the "modern era" without any significant event meriting that act. But baseball historians *did* draw a line at the turn of the century, and because of it he holds that rather important record.

Baseball historians named Chesbro as the American League pitcher for the all-time nine-player lineup of a team representing both leagues for what is known as the "Deadball Era," which are the years from 1900 to 1919 when the ball was manufactured differently and didn't travel as far off the bat as it does today. Ruth's 1919 slugging feat is even more impressive because that ball was still in use.

One of the weapons that made Chesbro so special in 1904 was a nasty spitball that he added to his repertoire prior to the 1902 season. He had learned how to throw the baffling pitch from a hurler named Elmer Stricklett when Chesbro was on a barnstorming tour in

California after the 1901 season. Chesbro was amazed how the pitch could suddenly drop or curve after some saliva had been applied to the ball. Stricklett played four major league seasons and won a total of 35 games, but the gift that he gave Chesbro enabled the pitcher to add another effective pitch to his already powerful fastball and make baseball history.

Stan Coveleski, another practictioner of the spitball during the early part of the 20th century, is a more comparable player than Koosman. Coveleski spent most of his playing career with the Cleveland Indians, joining them in 1916. Like Chesbro, he posted five seasons of 20 wins or more, but Coveleski never won more than 24 games. The Veterans Committee voted to give him entry to the Hall of Fame in 1969.

Coveleski played three more seasons than Chesbro and has 15 more career wins, yet Chesbro leads in complete games, 243 to 226. "Happy Jack" had the most wins and best winning percentage in each league, with the Pirates in 1902 and the Highlanders in 1904. Coveleski, a career American Leaguer, never accomplished that double once. Chesbro's career winning percentage is higher than Coveleski's .603 and his ERA of 2.68 is lower than the Indians' hurler.

The spitball was phased out of baseball when a rule was instituted following the 1920 season in which Cleveland's Ray Chapman had been killed by a spitball thrown by the Yankees' Carl Mays. Nobody could use the pitch for the first time, but pitchers who already employed it like Coveleski were grandfathered in relation to the rule, allowing them to continue throwing it until they retired.

It is unfortunate that Chesbro's epic 41-12 season was marred in the end by a wild pitch spitball that cost the Highlanders the pennant against Boston. On October 10, Chesbro was slotted to pitch the first of two final games of the season. The Highlanders needed to win both against the Red Sox to capture the pennant. With the score tied, 2-2, in the top of the ninth, Chesbro unleashed a spitball that missed the mark, getting away from the catcher and allowing Boston's Lou Criger to score the winning run.

North Adams, a former mill town that now features a state college and the Massachusetts Museum of Contemporary Art, is nestled at the base of the picturesque Berkshire Mountains, home of the state's tallest peak, Mount Greylock. One way of getting there from Eastern Massachusetts involves driving around the famous hairpin turn overlooking the Hoosac Valley.

The city honored Chesbro in 1971 and erected a plaque which sits near the entrance of Joe Wolfe Field there, but surprisingly there appears to be no other trace of Chesbro in his native city. At last check, the Heritage State Park Museum, which tells of the area's history, has exhibits about the building of the Hoosac railroad tunnel, as well as other exhibits depicting North Adams' past. Chesbro is conspicuously missing.

He was born on June 5, 1874, and lived in the Houghtonville section of the city. The family name was actually spelled Cheesbro. He was the fourth of five children born to Chad and Martha Jane (Fratenburg) Cheesbro. The second "e" was dropped in his early major league years.

Before gaining the name of "Happy Jack" he was called "Chad" growing up. The "Happy Jack" moniker seems to trace back to the time he played for a team sponsored by his former employer, the Middletown Asylum, a mental institution in New York. Some said the "Happy Jack" nickname related to his pleasant disposition, but it didn't really take hold until he had been playing professional ball for a few years, and it wasn't meant to be a compliment. Opposing players found he had had worked for a mental institution and gave him the name, implying he wasn't "all there" upstairs. Another theory about the origin of the nickname is that it was based on the look on his face when he delivered the ball, a look that some described as looking maniacal.

After playing for teams in Berkshire County, including one called the Houghtonville Nine, Chesbro pitched for several clubs in the minor leagues before being sold to the Pirates in 1899. Those stops included Albany (New York), Johnstown (Pennsylvania), Springfield (Massachusetts), and Roanoke and Richmond (Virginia). Chesbro's departure from Albany, Johnstown, and Roanoke were the result of the fact that either the club or league folded. In between the Roanoke and Richmond stops, Chesbro played for a semi-pro team in Cooperstown. It is believed he may be the only Hall of Famer to have actually played for a Cooperstown team.

After his outstanding seasons with Pittsburgh in 1901 and '02, the Highlanders made him a substantial offer of $4,500 in 1903, twice what he was making in Pittsburgh, that lured him to the American League. It was the Highlanders' first season in the American League, which had been established in 1901. By that time he was often called by another nickname, "Ches."

New York manager Clark Griffith wasn't an advocate of the spitball, but he gave Chesbro the green light to make it a part of his repertoire in 1904. That led to a 14-game winning streak and the historic season.

During that season he told *The Sporting News,* "I can make the spitball drop two inches or a foot and a half…The spitball is worked entirely by the thumb. The saliva one puts on the ball for the sole purpose of making the fingers slip off the ball first. Excepting the spitball, every ball that goes from the pitcher leaves the fingers last. In throwing curves the fingers do the work. By wetting the ball it leaves the fingers first and the thumb last, and the spitball could be rightly called the thumbball."

One of the reasons he mastered the spitball was he possessed both long fingers and a long arm, which allowed him to grip the ball well and throw it with great velocity. Pat McGrevey is given credit as teaching the finer points of pitching when Chesbro played for the hospital team. McGrevey believed Chesbro's physical characteristics helped him gain pitching success. These traits would aid him greatly, as he was not a physically imposing man, usually having a playing weight of 180 pounds and standing 5-feet, 9-inches tall.

Ty Cobb called the spitball a "freak pitch." Chesbro allowed Cobb's first career hit in 1905, but it is not known if he hit a spitball. He pitched the first game in the Highlanders' team history. He did get a chance to pitch for his home state team, throwing one game for the Red Sox in 1909, a loss, before retiring.

Ironically, and unfairly, Chesbro would be remembered by some as being the pitcher who threw away the pennant with that errant spitball in 1904, instead of the incredible season he turned in. He became somewhat of a Bill Buckner figure, much as the Giants' Fred

Merkle and Fred Snodgrass did a few years later after making mistakes, mental and physical, in important games.

Buckner's teammate, relief pitcher Bob Stanley, also comes to mind as someone who was ridiculed after throwing a damaging wild pitch, enabling the tying run to score in the same inning where Buckner shortly later made his famous World Series miscue. Like Chesbro's throw, that pitch was also debated about as to whether it was erroneously recorded as a wild pitch. Some argued it officially should have been recorded as a passed ball against Red Sox catcher Rich Gedman.

It would be 16 years before the Highlanders, then named the Yankees, would compete for a pennant again. Bill Dineen, the winning Red Sox pitcher in that historic final 1904 game against the Highlanders, was the only pitcher that season to beat Chesbro twice. Dineen also had an outstanding season, though his 23-14 record was eclipsed by Chesbro's.

"Happy Jack" took full responsibility for the wild pitch, though some blamed catcher Red Kleinow for letting the pitch get by him. Chesbro dwelled on the miscue in the offseason until Griffith told him to forget about it and "shut up." He took the advice to heart, winning 43 games over the next two seasons, but never came close to his 1904 statistics.

Then again, it was a memory that he couldn't fully shake, as he was often asked about it, even after leaving baseball. The infamous ball from that game against Boston reportedly resided in Scully's Café in North Adams as late as the 1990s. It is said that Chesbro gave the ball to his friend, proprietor Daniel Scully. It seems odd that Chesbro would have given the ball to Scully to put it on display when one considers how that pitch affected the rest of his life. Maybe he didn't know it was going to be put on display.

Chesbro had coached at Harvard College during his major league career, sometimes missing spring training to coach the Crimson. After he retired, he continued coaching at the college level. Several news reports indicated that he coached at Amherst College, but another report stated that it was actually at Massachusetts Agricultural College, which later became the University of Massachusetts.

He attempted a comeback in 1912, but he couldn't catch on with a professional club. Chesbro had to be content pitching for local semi-pro teams, which he did until he was 53. His last appearance on a Major League mound was in 1922 when he threw in a charity game. He served as a pitching coach for the Washington Senators in 1924 when his old manager Griffith asked him to join his staff.

Chesbro was back on his chicken farm in Conway, Massachusetts the following year, giving up professional baseball for good. He died on November 6, 1931 at 56. *The New York Times* noted his passing. His obituary reported that he had just eaten dinner and walked up a hill to attend to a problem with a spring that piped water to his farm. When he didn't return, his wife Mabel became concerned and went looking for him. She found him dead near the spring, due to what was believed to be a heart attack.

In 1939, Mabel tried to make the case that the fateful throw that was ruled a wild pitch should be officially changed to a passed ball in the record books. Knowing how her husband carried that with him until his death, it was her hope that she could give him some peace at long last. She was not successful in that effort. It remains officially a wild pitch.

Mabel and Jack never had children. He probably would have loved having a son to whom he could teach the game. He once said, "I would advise every boy to play professional baseball if he has the talent."

CHAPTER 10

MICKEY MANTLE

If you lived in New York during the 1950s and '60s there was one baseball player who shone above the rest. He was "The Natural"—not in a book or movie—but in person. During his playing days, Mickey Mantle owned New York. I happened to be one of those New Yorkers, spending part of my childhood living on Long Island before moving to Massachusetts in 1968, a few months after Mantle's final season.

The Yankees were THE team if you lived in that state. Of course, the Mets performed the "Miracle" a year later to begin seriously competing for New York's affections, but the Yankees always have been the more revered franchise, one that boasts 27 World Championships.

During his 18 seasons, Mantle played in 16 All-Star Games, was a member of seven World Series championship teams, captured three league Most Valuable Player Awards, won the Triple Crown, and in 1999 was named to the All-Century Team. Mantle's number 7 was worn by Little Leaguers with Big League dreams for many years.

I had dinner with "The Mick" the night prior to an autograph show in Sturbridge, Massachusetts in 1990, listening to his many stories.

10

"The Natural" In Person

MICKEY MANTLE SAT at a table the day before he was to sign autographs at a Baseball Collectors Show. Mantle did no more than 10 card shows a year and it was a coup for show promoter Kevin Huard to secure Mantle's appearance. Huard had been pursuing Mantle for a full year before he got his commitment to appear.

Mantle had some ground rules. He would not sign bats, uniforms, or statues. Huard said Joe DiMaggio stopped signing bats, driving the price up of those with his signature, and many of the leading players followed this practice. Mantle would sign 800 autographs over a two-day weekend period. The price was $35 for one item, plus a $5 admission fee to the show, which included other former stars such as the Braves' Eddie Mathews and Johnny Sain.

The youthful face was gone. It showed his 58 years. He had a long battle with alcoholism and five years later he would pass away, a victim of liver cancer. His father, Mutt Mantle, had died of Hodgkin's disease at 40 in 1952. That disease also took his grandfather and two uncles. So he had a sense of his own mortality at an early age. He once said, "If I had known that I was going to live so long I would have taken better care of myself."

Alcoholism affected his family as well. His wife Merilyn and three of his four sons sought treatment for the disease, as did Mickey himself. Two of his four sons died young. Billy died at 36 of heart problems linked to substance abuse. He had also acquired the Hodgkin's disease that had plagued Mantle's family. Mickey Mantle Jr. succumbed to liver cancer at 47.

By the time Mantle was 63, the years of abusing his body with alcohol caught up with him, as doctors performed a liver transplant in June of 1995. He died two months later. The Hodgkin's disease he feared never afflicted him, but his friend and home run champion Roger Maris died of it 10 years earlier. He was only 51.

On the day before the autograph show, the former Yankee great was in full control and in good spirits. It seemed that he enjoyed nothing more than reliving the old glory days.

He was not the same type of hitter as his two heroes: Stan Musial and Ted Williams, the latter being Mantle's greatest idol.

In his autobiography, "The Mick" he wrote, "They were every bit as strong as I am. The difference is that they were always trying to meet the ball, while I was always trying to kill it. If you swing for distance, you almost have to have the bat in motion before the pitch is even released. You can't chop at it and expect it to go 500 feet. You take a full cut and generate a little extra power, praying you don't miss."

Reminded of that statement, he told a story that further showed the difference between Williams and himself, aside from the fact that Mantle was a switch hitter. Williams was a true student of the game, later writing a book about his scientific approach to hitting. Mantle didn't think about hitting that way. He swung from his heels, watched what happened, and didn't spend much time thinking about exactly how he swung at a ball.

"I remember that I was at an All-Star Game and (Williams') locker was right next to mine," Mantle said. "Some people have told this story and said that I walked up to him and asked him about hitting. Actually, he came up to me and started questioning me about it.

"Williams said, 'When you swing right-handed do you pull one hand like this, and guide the other hand like this? And when you swing left-handed do you pull one-hand like this, and guide the other hand like this?' Well, I just looked at him (after Williams demonstrated swings). I never really thought about it. I think I went 0 for 40 after the All-Star Game before I started hitting again."

Mantle's approach to hitting resulted in a lot of home runs, 536 in all, but it also resulted in a lot of strikeouts. He fanned 1,710 times in his 18-year career. He once asked his friend and teammate Whitey Ford why he was striking out so much and Ford said, "I think you're closing your eyes before you swing." When he did connect, boy did he connect. Many people still remember the titanic home run he hit in early April of 1953 against Chuck Stobbs in Washington's Griffith Stadium.

Mel Allen, the longtime Yankee announcer, described it this way: *"Here's the pitch. There's a tremendous drive going into deep left field. It's going, going, it's going OVER the bleachers, and over the sign atop the bleachers and into the yards of houses across the street. It's got to be one of the longest home runs I've ever seen hit. How ABOUT that!"*

Allen later commented that the Yankees' publicity director, Red Patterson, had used a tape measure to determine how far the ball had travelled. The answer was 565 feet.

But fewer people may remember another home run Mantle hit in 1963 that nearly left the old Yankee Stadium. The blast came off Kansas City's Bill Fischer, who later served as a pitching coach for the Red Sox.

"That was the hardest ball I ever hit," Mantle said. "It hit the façade and was about three feet from going out. The one in Griffith Stadium was helped by the wind, but this one just kept going on a line."

Later, some people from the Massachusetts Institute of Technology came to Yankee Stadium to try to determine how far the ball would have gone had it not hit the façade. They estimated that it would have travelled 600 feet, so THAT may have been the longest home run ever hit.

Every hitter has problems against certain pitchers. For Mantle, one of those pitchers was the Red Sox' Walt Masterson, a pitcher with a 78-100 lifetime record. "I just couldn't hit him," he said. "Who would have thought a guy like Walt Masterson could get me out so much?"

Actually, Masterson's record is misleading. During the prime of his career, from 1947-51, he had allowed less than four runs a game and had the misfortune of pitching for several poor teams.

Another pitcher he had trouble hitting was Leroy "Satchel" Paige, the Negro League ballplayer who followed Jackie Robinson into the Major Leagues in 1948.

Mantle remembered that in the early '50s the St. Louis Browns broke an 18-game Yankee winning streak, saying that the loss sent the Yankees into a nine-game losing skid.

"It was funny because we were probably one of the best teams ever, and they were probably one of the worst teams," he said. "We lost four straight to them."

During one of the games in that series, he faced Paige, who Mantle said "must have been 80" at the time. Actually, he was in his mid-40s. In a late inning situation, with two men on base and two outs, Mantle tried to bunt against him with two strikes, fouling it off and ending the inning.

"I walked over to the corner of the dugout and sat down," Mantle said. "(Manager) Casey (Stengel) came to me and said, 'Son, if I want you to bunt I'll let you know.'"

Mantle's memory of that Browns series is a bit off. New York, after losing the series opener, won five of its next six games, including the last three against the Browns. It was *then* the Yankees lost nine straight. Chalk it up to The Passage of Time—but his recollection of the failed bunt is completely accurate.

After his father died, Stengel became a great influence on the life of the Oklahoma boy. "He was like a second father to me," Mantle said.

Yet Stengel created some problems for him when he first came into the Majors. "He kept calling me 'phenom' and comparing me to Babe Ruth and (Joe) DiMaggio," Mantle said. "I was just trying to make it in the big leagues."

Like Boston's Carl Yastrzemski, who felt the pressure of replacing Williams, Mantle felt the same way when the resident Yankee God, DiMaggio, retired after his rookie season. Both men dealt with the pressure well, but it wasn't easy.

Stengel once said, "The secret to being a good manager is keeping the five guys who hate you away from the four guys who haven't made up their minds yet." Mantle said he hadn't heard that comment, but added, "That sounds like something he would say."

Sometimes the Yankees acquired a former great player who was finishing out his career, like Johnny Sain. Once a standout starting pitcher for the Boston Braves, Sain became a star reliever for the Yankees from '52-'54, leading the league in saves in '54 with 26.

"We'd get guys like Johnny (Sain) and Johnny Mize near the end of their careers and they'd end up having two or three great years for us," Mantle said. Sain was a member of three Yankee World Series championship teams in his four years in pinstripes, while Mize—acquired from the Giants—was a member of Series championship teams in all five of his seasons in the Bronx.

Sounds a little like the way Red Auerbach resurrected some careers with the Celtics.

Though he had some fine seasons in his early years, Mantle didn't feel secure with the Yankees and certain that he could be an all-time great until 1956 when he won the Triple Crown, hitting 52 home runs, collecting 132 RBI, logging a lofty .353 batting average. He is the last Triple Crown winner to lead in all three categories in both leagues.

Mantle holds the highest OPS, determined by on-base percentage and slugging average, in baseball history. He played in 12 Word Series, with the Yankees winning seven, and also won a Gold Glove. He holds Series records in home runs (18), RBIs (40), and in four other batting categories, and hit .300 or more in 10 seasons.

Considered the greatest switch hitter in baseball history, Mantle was one of those rare players to have success batting from both sides of the plate. His father and grandfather encouraged him to be a switch hitter, one being a right-handed thrower, the other a lefty. Mantle got plenty of practice as a boy hitting balls from both slants.

People sometimes just remember Mantle in the later stages in his career, when knee injuries hobbled him. Actually, he was once one of the fastest players in the league. He could move from home plate to first base in 3.1 seconds. He never had more than 21 stolen bases in a season, but that was more because Stengel didn't want him to steal too much. With the Yankee offense the way it was, why take chances?

When he left the game, he had the highest stolen base percentage in baseball history.

The '61 Yankees once were ranked by *The Sporting News* as the second greatest team of all-time, behind Ruth's '27 Yankees. Like all great teams, the Yankees of Mantle, Maris, and Ford always had a quiet confidence.

"If it was in the seventh inning and we were behind we knew that we could win," Mantle said. "It's unbelievable how we won by scoring runs late. We could just turn it on and off like that. It was like, 'OK, guys, it's time we started doing something.' "

Along with his 536 home runs, he finished his career with a .298 batting average and 1,509 runs batted in. After a '68 season that saw him bat .237 with only 18 home runs he decided to leave the baseball stage.

That season was the "Year of the Pitcher," as Detroit's Denny McClean won 31 games. Cleveland's Luis Tiant posted a microscopic 1.60 ERA and a 21-9 record. Yastrzemski was the only American League batter to hit above .300, finishing at .301. Oakland's Danny Cater, who was traded by the Yankees to Boston four years later in the infamous Sparky Lyle deal, placed second at .290. The Cardinals' Bob Gibson threw 13 shutouts. Yet, Mantle knew it was time to make his exit shortly before spring training began in '69.

He told the media then, "I've been thinking about retiring. I got into Fort Lauderdale last night and I talked to Ralph Houk for about an hour on the phone. Then I had breakfast with (team president) Mike Burke this morning and we all three decided it was about time that we give somebody else a chance to help the ballclub."

In the ensuing years, the Yankees found how hard it was to replace the man whose nickname was the "Commerce Comet," referring to his Oklahoma roots and speed on the basepaths. In a way, he was like Halley's Comet, which appears to the naked eye only once every 75 years.

He truly was "The Natural."

AUTHOR'S NOTE
AND ACKNOWLEDGEMENTS

THE WRITING AND production of a book is a collaborative effort. For me, the vision of this book came shortly after I left the *Fitchburg-Leominster Sentinel & Enterprise* in 1991. I want to thank the *Sentinel & Enterprise* and particularly my managing editor, Ann Connery Frantz, for their support and encouragement of this writing project.

For me, writing this book has been a long and winding road. There have been a lot of starts and stops, with momentum building in the last two years when the manuscript was finally completed.

I want to thank all the legends who took time out to talk to me and for their cordial manner.

My brothers, Brian and Dan Daly—both writers themselves—were greatly helpful in reviewing the manuscript and giving many suggestions that improved the text.

They also assisted me in developing the book title, as did Steve Castle, a friend and former colleague from my *Sentinel & Enterprise* days. Also thanks to my sister, Ellen Bell, for her support, and to John Gearan and Mike Richard for their words of praise found on the book's back cover.

One thing that came across when doing interviews with legends such as these is that they are human beings who happen to have talents superior to most of the people in their profession. They couldn't have been nicer to me, somebody who was not a Boston beat writer and who was meeting them for the first time.

I wish I could have met Rocky Marciano, who retired from the ring the same year I was born. His story is a compelling one. Thanks to Dino Colombo, Todd Petti, and others who helped me bring Rocky back to life in this book's chapter.

Glenn Lawson, reference specialist of the North Adams Public Library, was instrumental in giving me access to a file there which contains all things Jack Chesbro. I was pleased to find so many old newspaper clippings and articles, helping me to construct Chesbro's story as it should be told.

Thanks to Kevin Huard for making my meeting and interview with Mickey Mantle possible, and also an unexpected side meeting with Johnny Sain.

Jamaal Dockery, a proud 2018 graduate of Mount Wachusett Community College's Graphic Arts Program, did a wonderful job with the illustrations and book cover design. I was fortunate that Jamaal was available to work on these tasks immediately after graduation. Thanks to Professor Leslie Cullen, director of the program, for making me aware of Jamaal's talent and arranging for our meeting.

Also, thanks to Kirsten Ringer and Lisa Jones of my publisher, Outskirts Press, and everyone there who helped make the final published book a reality.

Finally, a tip of the hat to some of my personal sportswriting heroes, beginning with Paul Gallico, a legend from a bygone era. He is followed by more modern scribes such as Frank Deford, Roger Angell, Peter Gammons, Leigh Montville, and my brother Dan, a longtime newspaper columnist who has written two fine books about the history of the National Football League.

I stand on the shoulders of these heroes who have influenced my development as a writer.

ABOUT THE AUTHOR

CHRISTOPHER DALY IS a former sportswriter and editor for the *Fitchburg-Leominster Sentinel & Enterprise*, a daily newspaper in Central Massachusetts, and has been honored by the New England Associated Press New Executives for sportswriting excellence. He has also written numerous articles on a wide variety of topics for the *Worcester (Mass.) Telegram and Gazette*.

Born on Long Island and raised there and in Massachusetts, he has been an enthusiast of teams from both New York and Boston, whose legendary sports figures are profiled in this book.

He began writing and broadcasting sports at North Adams State College, now known as the Massachusetts College of Liberal Arts, where he received a bachelor's degree in history and state teacher's certification. He did radio play-by-play for the school's men's basketball's games. Mr. Daly taught history at St. Mary's Junior-Senior High School in Worcester, and has lectured on history at local venues, including The Gardner Museum. A licensed real estate broker, he owns Daly's Property Shoppe in Gardner, Massachusetts.

The one-time city tennis champion and frequent Fenway Park and Boston Garden spectator resides in Gardner. He also wrote part of this book at his retreat on Cape Cod.

CPSIA information can be obtained
at www.ICGtesting.com
Printed in the USA
BVHW072202201219
567391BV00001B/40/P